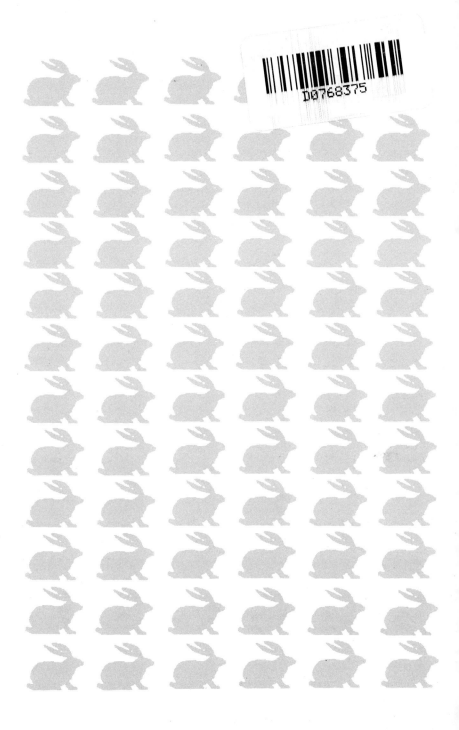

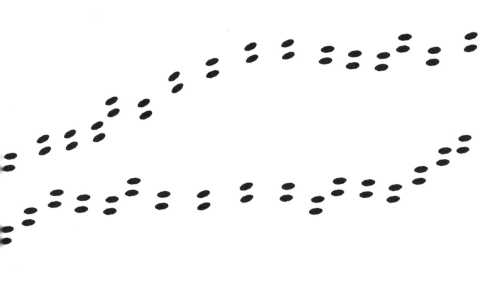

STALKING THE WILD SOLUTION

A PROBLEM FINDING APPROACH
TO CREATIVE PROBLEM SOLVING

ARTHUR B. VAN GUNDY, PH.D.

Copyrights & Permissions

- *Famous People; Al & Jimmy; Cars; Celebrities; Farm Animals; Farm House; More Little Guys; Skylines; Space/Race; Statues* art from Click Art PERSONAL GRAPHICS, an electronic image portfolio from the Click Art series by T/Maker Company, Mountain View, CA. Copyright© 1984. All rights reserved.

- Excerpt on Page 4: From **The Evolution Of Physics: The Growth Of Ideas From Early Concepts To Relativity And Quanta** by Albert Einstein & Leopold Infeld. Copyright© 1938, Albert Einstein and Leopold Infeld. Reprinted by permission of Simon and Schuster, Inc., publishers.

- Excerpt on Page 7: From **Productive Thinking** by M. Wertheimer. Copyright© 1945 by Valentin Wertheimer. Reprinted by permission of Harper & Row, publishers.

CONTENTS

Our favorite TV detective, Mike Dallas, sits behind his splintered, faded desk with his feet propped up on a World War II surplus filing cabinet. A bottle of Old Rot Gut rests by his left elbow. As he absent-mindedly thumbs through a well-worn copy of a girlie magazine, he inhales a few swigs from his glass.

Hearing footsteps, Mike looks up and sees Bruno, the notorious killer. His hulking frame obscures the little light that filters in from the dimly-lit hallway outside Mike's office. Dispensing with all formalities, Bruno tells Mike he is going to get him for "sending him up the river." As he speaks, Bruno's eyes begin to glaze and his face reddens.

"You'll be dead before sundown, you dirty rat!" Bruno spits out the words as if they were watermelon seeds. "You can count on today being your last!"

Apparently unfazed, Mike counters with a clever witticism, watches Bruno spin on his heels as he starts to leave, and returns to his booze and magazine. Moments later, he glances out his window at the teeming city below, gulps down the rest of his bottle, and calls to his secretary. "Stella, bring me my .44. I've got some business to take care of."

Our hero clearly faces a rather difficult problem situation. In fact, you might even say he has a dilemma. If he chases after Bruno he risks being killed. Bruno will be looking for him, so he is in even greater danger. If he leaves town or goes to the police, he risks losing face. Macho TV detectives just don't run or hide under police protection.

After evaluating his dilemma, our hero decides to define his problem as: "In what ways might I avoid being killed by Bruno by sundown?" He decides that the only possible solution is to chase after Bruno and "run him into the ground." Is this a rational solution? Of course not. Is this solution likely to sustain viewer interest with high drama, tension, conflict, and the scream of tires? Of course. To leave town or seek police protection would be just plain boring to the viewer. Even worse, running away would not be macho. Analyzed in this way, our hero has somewhat limited options. By defining his problem as avoiding death by sundown and his solution as capturing or possibly killing Bruno (with all necessary blood, violence, and general mayhem), our detective has locked himself into a prescribed course of action. He used the first problem definition which popped into his head. As a result, he was guided automatically to what appeared to be the only "logical solution."

Although this solution may have solved a problem (namely, maintaining interest) for the show's producers and the viewers, the solution is not ideal for our hero. Only one "horn" of his dilemma will be resolved: He will save face and preserve his macho image. He still must deal with the other "horn." Charging after Bruno involves a high risk of being killed by exposing himself to someone who should be anticipating his every reaction. Thus, our hero quickly developed a solution, but it may not have been a high quality solution.

Instead of immediately assuming he had found his problem, our hero might have spent a little more time analyzing the situation. He might have been better off seeking a problem definition which could have resolved both horns of his dilemma—a solution allowing him to save face while, at the same time, decreasing the odds of being killed by Bruno. What our hero really needed was a "problution"—a cross between a problem and a solution. That is, he needed to clarify and structure his problem to such an extent that a high quality solution would emerge as the best possible outcome.

Our TV hero did what many of us do when confronted by difficult problem situations. He immediately began generating a solution without a fully-developed understanding of the problem. He began with the idea-finding stage of the creative problem-solving process instead of taking time to gather relevant facts and determine the nature of the problem he needed to solve. According to the famous educator, John Dewey, "discovering a problem is the first step in knowing" (1938). We cannot learn much about our lives or our problems unless we first understand our problems. We may think we understand them when we first encounter problems, but this often is not the case. Information may be overlooked which is not always apparent at the outset. Without this information, it is not likely that a high quality solution can be achieved. With this information, however, achieving such a solution often is the easiest part of problem solving. Albert Einstein vividly illustrated this point in commenting on scientific problem solving:

> *The formulation of a problem is often more essential than its solution which may be merely a matter of mathematical or experimental skill. To raise new questions, new possibilities, to regard old questions from a new angle, requires creative imagination and marks real advance in science.*
> (Einstein & Infeld, 1938, p. 95)

In his statement, Einstein highlights the importance of questioning in problem solving. Because our TV hero neglected to ask questions about his dilemma, he took a chance on risking his life. By asking how he might avoid being killed by Bruno, the detective severely limited his options. He may have been better off asking a more abstract question such as, "In what ways might I make myself invisible to Bruno?"

This revised question provides a slightly different perspective on his dilemma and leaves open a variety of solution options. For example, our hero might adopt different disguises while chasing Bruno. Or, he might hire

> "The formulation of a problem often is more important than its solution."
>
> -- A. E.

other detectives to chase Bruno while orchestrating the search from the background. Both solutions would allow our hero to save face and resolve the dilemma. He also could think of other problem restatements and use them to suggest solutions. Thus, he might redefine his problem as: "In what ways might I get Bruno to come to me?" This reversal suggests the idea of developing a trap and luring Bruno to it with the expectation of an easy "hit" on our hero. Our detective, of course, would be prepared and right would triumph.

The importance of questioning in problem solving can be illustrated further by a story developed by Dillon, Schwartz, and Smilansky (Getzels, 1975). It demonstrates nicely how problem finding often is more important than idea finding.

A car travels down a deserted country road and blows a tire. Upon opening the car's trunk, the occupants discover that the jack is missing. This prompts them to pose their problem as: "In what ways might we obtain a jack?" One remembers a service station they passed a few miles back and they all decide to walk to it and borrow a jack. After they leave, another car, coming from the opposite direction, also blows a tire. When the occupants of this car open their trunk, they also discover (quite conveniently for this story) that the jack is missing. This group defines their problem as: "In what ways might we raise the car?" One notices a barn nearby with a pulley for lifting hay bales to the loft. They push the car to the barn, raise the car with the pulley, and change the tire. As they drive off, the occupants of the first car are still walking to get a jack from the service station.

Getzels notes that using the pulley to change the tire was a clever solution. However, a better comment might be: "What a clever question!" The high quality so-

lution used by the second car's occupants was a direct result of the quality of the problem question they posed and the problem they found. The occupants of the first car, in contrast, limited their solution options by defining their problem as how to get a jack. In this case, discovering a problem was far more important than discovering a solution.

Problem situations with many different solution possibilities usually can be resolved best by spending some time discovering or creating problems. Once the problem finder locates or develops the best problem for the situation, solutions will present themselves almost as if by magic.

We often assume that we know what the problem is when, in fact, this rarely is the case. We need to question our problem situations to increase our understanding of them. As Wertheimer (1959) observed:

> The problem with its solution function as parts of a large expanding realm. Here the function of thinking is not just solving an actual problem but discovering, envisaging, going into deeper questions. Often in great discoveries the most important thing is that a certain question is found. Envisaging, putting the productive question is often more important, often a greater achievement than solution of a set question. (p. 123).

As will be seen shortly, asking the productive question is not only important to problem solving, it also is the key to effective problem solving whenever creative solutions are required. Finding the "right" problem is equivalent to finding the "right" solution. Problems and solutions are close relatives and do not always need to be separated for effective problem solving.

Defining a Problem

To understand how problem finding differs from problem solving, it is first necessary to understand what a problem is. Many definitions of problems have been proposed, but not all of them are adequate. In fact, many of these definitions contribute very little to an understanding of either problem finding or problem solving.

Let's start with the dictionary. Webster's dictionary (1979) defines a problem as a "question proposed for solution or consideration; a question, matter, situation or person that is perplexing or difficult." This definition describes a problem as a perplexing question for which a solution is sought. However, it is not a sufficient definition, since it is much too general for our purposes. Just think of some of the problems people face: In what ways might I get my children to pick up their toys? In what ways might I become more satisfied with my job? In what ways might I convince my boss I deserve a raise? All of these problems can be viewed as perplexing. However, perplexity alone cannot structure or guide analysis of our problems or help us generate solutions. Something more is needed.

How about this definition? "A problem arises when a living creature has a goal but does not know how the goal is to be reached" (Duncker, 1945, p. 1). A little better. With this definition, at least, one aspect of a problem situation has been specified. Implied here is the notion that a problem exists when a goal is blocked. That is, you know what you want, but you are uncertain how to get it. For example, you know you want a raise, but you don't know how to ask for it. The only thing missing from this definition is the current state of your problem. Although it is implied, explicit recognition of the current state in our definition might result in greater understanding.

Adding this extra dimension results in the following definition of a problem: A gap between what is and what should be (e.g., Newell, Shaw & Simon, 1958; MacCrimmon, 1974). This way of looking at a problem acknowledges an initial problem state (what is), a desired problem state (what should be), and the existence of some perceived difference between the two. You cannot walk into your child's room without the assistance of a bulldozer (what is) and you would like the floor of the room to be free of toys (what should be). Note that the gap or difference in this situation is what you perceive it to be according to your goal preferences—i.e., you don't want the floor littered with toys. However, someone else might not mind the toys on the floor. This person would not have a problem, since the initial state is, presumably, identical to the desired state. If there is no perceived gap, there can't be a problem.

For most purposes, this definition of a problem will be adequate. Resolving such problems is just a matter of applying operators to reduce or eliminate the gap between what is and what should be. In conventional problem solving, the process of altering a gap involves a

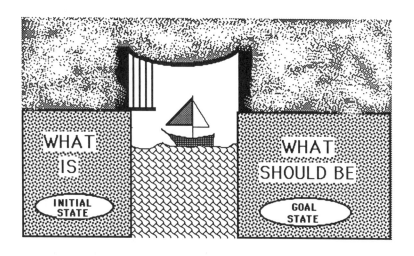

search for solutions. A rather neat and tidy situation appears to exist with this definition: Define what your current and desired problem states are and develop ways (solutions) to make the current state more like the desired state.

Unfortunately, problem solving in real life isn't always this simple. Sometimes we know what is, but not what should be; sometimes we know what should be, but not what is; and sometimes we are not sure of what is or what should be, but we have plenty of solutions available nevertheless (e. g., money is a solution to a lot of problems waiting to be found).

Whenever such problem states exist, problems can be classified as ill-defined or ill-structured (MacCrimmon & Taylor, 1976). In contrast to well-defined problems, ill-defined problems can be solved best using creative solutions. Well-defined problems, by comparison, require routine types of solutions, since the problem is structured sufficiently well that no solutions need to be created. Existing solutions that have worked in the past usually will be adequate. Because well-defined problems do not need to be found, ill-defined problems will be the primary concern of this book.

In dealing with ill-defined problems, our preferences and perceptions about current and desired problem states may change over time. Moreover, the availability and validity of problem information also may change over time as new information becomes available.

For example, you might experience some general dissatisfaction in your job. As you analyze your feelings, you note that you are unhappy about some specific job tasks (what is), but you are uncertain about exactly how things could be improved (what should be). Or, you may know exactly what it is you want out of your job, but not know specifically what bothers you about the current state of your position. However, as you gain more experience in your job and the job itself changes, your perceptions might change. You also may begin to see it as an extremely vague problem in which you are uncertain about both the current and desired states. How you deal with such problems depends on your perceptions at a particular time. Your perceptions, in turn, will be determined by your prior experiences with similar problems and the knowledge you have about them.

Although defining a problem as a gap between current and desired states will be adequate for most purposes, it does have one weakness I noted previously: It results in a static definition. Since most problems are not static, a dynamic definition would seem to be more appropriate. This is especially important for problem situations which are highly changeable. Problems which change very little—especially those that change only in small increments over an extended period of time—can be defined more appropriately using a static definition.

However, I believe that the majority of problem situations we encounter are dynamic. They may remain relatively stable for short periods, but the shifting nature of our complex environment frequently produces rather drastic changes in our problems. As new information becomes available, we need to assess the validity of old information and develop new ways of looking at our problems.

Unfortunately, we often persist in holding onto our initial perceptions of problem situtations. We may fail to search for new information or continually evaluate the quality of the information we do possess. Too often the tendency is to state problems as unchangeable givens and work from there toward a solution. Just as the occupants of the first car did in the car jack illustration, we may tend to assume we know what is and what should be and proceed accordingly. We often neither seek new information nor examine our initial assumptions.

These failings of static problem definitions suggest that we should look for a more dynamic definition. Rather than defining a problem in terms of our existing (and frequently inadequate) behaviors, we might be better off if we looked for a more prescriptive definition. That is, we need a definition reflecting what we should do and, at the same time, at least imply that defining a problem is a dynamic process.

John Dewey (1938), provided a definition coming close to meeting these requirements. To Dewey, a problem "represents the partial transformation . . . of a problematic situation into a determinate situation" (p. 108). A problem is not just a gap between two states. It also is an ongoing change process involving the continual transformation of the problem states.

It could easily be argued that Dewey's definition describes problem solving more than it does a problem. The notion of movement toward a goal in his definition also is used in most classical definitions which describe the problem-solving process as moving from one state to another (e.g., Reitman, 1964). However, Dewey's use of the word "represents" suggests that a problem is dynamic—that the states of a problem are constantly changing. Our perceptions of a problem symbolize this state of change. In other words, it might be better to view a problem as something in a state of becoming rather than something that is.

Viewed this way, I would define a problem as a set of ongoing perceptions held about a constantly changing gap between a desired and existing state. Resolving a problem defined in this manner requires constant awareness about the nature of a problem situation from one time to another. It also requires searching for new information and re-examining old information. Because a problem is dynamic, our perceptions about it and the actions we take to deal with it also must be dynamic.

When compared with more static problem definitions, a dynamic definition has several advantages. First, it helps avoid confusing symptoms and causes. By locking in on one concrete definition, the static definition specifies what is symptom and what is cause. The dynamic definition, in contrast, allows you to consider many different symptoms and causes until you can locate the "real" problem. Second, a dynamic approach makes it easier to consider new information, since no fixed boundaries are established at the outset. A third advantage of a dynamic definition is that it allows you to view your problems in relation to the larger problem situation—to see the "big picture." Finally, a dynamic definition is well-suited for dealing with unexpected environmental changes. Because outside changes can affect how you perceive a problem, a flexible definition makes it easier to incorporate new information with your set of ongoing problem perceptions.

Although these advantages seem to make a good case for a dynamic definition of a problem, there is at least one disadvantage that should be mentioned. Viewing problems as dynamic makes it difficult to achieve closure on a problem and develop a solution to resolve the situation. When you view your problem as being in a continual state of flux, you may feel that very little progress is being made toward developing a solution. At some point, you need to state: "This is my problem as I see it and I need to solve it now." You can't continue to collect information and redefine it indefinitely. Nevertheless, a dynamic view of problems makes it easy to do just that.

In many situations, this difficulty will take care of itself. The time available to deal with a problem may be limited and force you to select a stable definition. Or, other resources you need to solve the problem may be available only at certain times and force closure on a definition. For example, I currently have administrative responsibilities requiring problem solutions to be developed within certain periods of time, using only limited funds. I usually don't have the option of unlimited time, since I am responsible to higher authorities (who also must operate under time and resource constraints).

In spite of this disadvantage of a dynamic definition, there is a silver lining. If we assume that we should use a flexible definition and that we operate under various resource constraints, then we can turn this disadvantage into an advantage. We can use this disadvantage to help resolve our problems. If we view dealing with a dynamic problem definition as problem finding, then we can use the process to help achieve a solution. Specifically, by continually adding new information to our problem definitions, we eventually may reach a point where the problem is so structured that a solution will pop right out.

Problem Finding and Problem Solving

We normally do not seek problems because of boredom or lack of problems to solve. Most of our problems have a way of finding us. After all, aren't there enough problems in the world without actively seeking more?

If you reflect upon your life, I am sure that you could develop a seemingly endless list of problems you have encountered. You probably resolved some relatively quickly, while others tended to resist solution. You may still be dealing with many problems first encountered years ago. Meanwhile, new problems continue to crop up and demand your attention. Most of us have more problems than we realistically can expect to resolve.

The number of problems we have to deal with, however, has very little to do with problem finding as I described it earlier. The problems we need to find lurk within broad problem situations waiting to be clarified and redefined. These broad situations usually are presented to us as ambiguous messes from which we must extract one or more initial problem definitions.

The definitions we extract depend on our particular understanding of the broader situation. Our ability to find a problem is influenced directly by this understanding. The more information we have about a broad problem situation, the more precise our definitions will be. Thus, solving problems is a matter of finding our "real" problems, based upon our understanding of the broader problem situation (Sims, 1979). What is real is, of course, relative and will vary from person to person.

If you have considerable knowledge about this broader situation and believe you understand it well, you will be very close to a solution and should have little difficulty finding the "real" problem. All you need do is apply a solution. Quite often this can be done with routine procedures, since this type of problem will be fairly well-defined. However, if you only have a limited understanding of the broad problem situation, you will need to seek information to help transform your understanding into a solution.

Using information to increase understanding of a problem is the basic mechanism of problem finding. Each time you add information about either the current or desired states of a problem situation, you are redefining the situation. The problem gradually will increase in structure until you "see" the solution you need. Thus, the primary task of problem finding is to change ill-defined problems into well-defined ones. The simple reason for this is that a well-defined problem is a solution. Once you understand a problem, you have solved it.

The metamorphosis involved in changing problems into solutions has been long recognized as the key to successful problem solving. As early as 1945, Duncker noted that "what is really done in any solution of problems consists in formulating the problem more productively" (p. 9). De Bono (1971) reinforced and extended this view by observing that: "Once one has an accurate definition of the problem, he is very close to the solution" (p. 168).

Based upon the preceding discussion, we now can define problem finding as an ongoing set of activities used to clarify current and desired states so the perceived difference between the states can be reduced using routine procedures. Put another way, problem finding is the process of transforming ill-structured problems (ISPs) into well-structured problems (WSPs). Note how this view of problem finding differs from my previous definition of a problem as a set of ongoing perceptions held about a constantly changing gap between a desired and existing state. A problem is how you perceive a situation; problem finding is how you act to clarify those perceptions.

A logical question at this point would be: "How are problems and problem finding related to problem solving?" The answer lies in the previous definitions of problems and problem finding. When we encounter a broad problem situation, we first need to spend some time becoming aware of the specific problem of interest to us. We do this by placing temporary boundaries around sets of elements in the broader situation. That is, we need to develop a continually changing perception of what is and what should be (the problem). In the process of doing this, we should attempt to build on our earlier perceptions and clarify the problem states and their relationship to each other (problem finding). As the states and the nature of their relationship become more and more clarified, our understanding increases.

However, all of these activities take time and other resources. We eventually have to settle for a problem definition that best captures our understanding at a particular point in the process. When this occurs, we use our current perception of the problem states as the gap needing to be reduced. This is where problem solving comes in.

In relation to the previous discussion, problem solving can be defined as the process of closing or reducing the gap between current and desired problem states. In most conventional problem-solving approaches, this gap is reduced by applying one or more solutions and then checking to see if the reduction has been successful (e.g., means-ends analysis as described by Newell & Simon, 1972). Problem finding involves essentially the same process, but no assumptions are made about the validity of the problem states. That is, not only are different solutions tried out, but different problem states also may be experimented with.

For example, in the car jack problem, the occupants of the first car defined their problem as a gap between not having a jack and needing a jack. They used the only "logical" solution: obtain a jack by walking back into town to the service station. No problem finding was used in this case except to assume that the problem already was found. In contrast, the occupants of the second car used problem finding and solve the same problem of a flat tire by clarifing the general problem situation until a solution emerged. The information they used involved noting that the car needed to be raised to change the tire. Thus clarified, the problem became one of simply closing the gap between the car not being raised and the car needing to be raised.

This redefinition of "In what ways might we raise the car?", in effect, became the solution. No further redefinitions were needed since a solution was self-evident to this group of individuals: Use the pulley from the barn to raise the car. The car's occupants could have redefined the problem further as: "In what ways might we use the pulley to raise the car?", although this would have been unnecessary (assuming that they all were knowledgeable and physiclly able to use the pulley). The problem was clarified sufficiently well so no further redefinitions were required.

The occupants of both cars used problem solving, but only the occupants of the second car used problem finding to redefine their problem to such an extent that a high quality solution emerged. By taking the time to analyze the problem and view it from a different perspective, they were able to produce a much more efficient and less time consuming solution than walking back into town.

Most of the preceding discussion can be summarized by stating that to stalk a solution is to find a problem. Our search for problem solutions is really a search for problems that capture best our needs, given the constraints operating on us. Once we find the "right" problem (for us) in a broader problem situation, our problem will be resolved. We will understand the problem states well enough to know how to reduce the gap between the states. Thus, stalking the wild solution is a matter of redefining our initial problem statements until one redefinition presents itself as a solution. As I noted earlier, I have termed this product a "problution," to symbolize the close relationship between problems and solutions. This concept of problutions will be discussed in more detail in Chapter Three.

Importance of Problem Finding

Problem finding is important because most of us tend to be solution-minded rather than problem-minded (Maier, 1963). Through conditioning in our institutions and within society, we have been trained to think of solutions to problems. The simple equation presented to us is: "Here is the problem, now you come up with the solution." We tend to treat most of the problems we face as givens. The solution becomes our primary goal when, in fact, the problem is really where we should be directing our efforts. As Thelen (1972) notes in discussing the educational system, schools tend to view education as "a process that only begins with someone else's statement of the problem." Perhaps schools should place some emphasis upon developing that problem definition.

Dealing with these presented problems, while important, is not nearly as important as dealing with problems that must be discovered or invented. Presented problems frequently can be resolved using algorithms or recipes guaranteeing a solution (e.g., most mathematical problems). Discovered or invented problems, in contrast, typically are ill-structured and require creative solutions. The only way high quality creative solutions can be achieved is through the use of problem finding. We must know where we are before we can begin the journey to where we want to be.

Although many writers have recognized the importance of problem finding, relatively little empirical research has been published to document its importance. Perhaps the best known studies were conducted by Getzels and Csikszentmihalyi (1964; 1965) and Csikszentmihalyi and Getzels (1970) who investigated the relationship between problem finding and artistic creativity.

The researchers asked artists to produce a drawing using various objects placed on a table in front of them.

The drawings were judged independently by a panel of well-known artists and art critics. The results indicated that artists who approached the task with no set problem in mind and who avoided using predetermined artistic patterns produced more original drawings than those who began with a predetermined approach. The researchers noted that artists who did not use a predetermined approach found problems rather than using ones that may have been presented to them previously. It is significant to note that many of the artists whose works were judged higher in originality spent considerable time manipulating the objects.

Similar results were obtained by Moore (1985) in a replication of this research, using middle school students who were asked to produce a written work. As in the Getzels and Csikszentmihalyi studies, the students were provided with various objects which they could choose to use as stimuli for their writing. Students judged to be creative tended to produce more original writings than the noncreatives. In general, there appeared to be a positive relationship between problem finding and originality of the final products.

Although more research clearly is needed, there would seem to be little doubt that problem finding is an important element in dealing with ill-structured problems. The ambiguous and often-changing nature of such problems requires that their problem states be understood. Without such understanding, there can be no hope of achieving a high quality solution.

Overview of the Stalking Process

Stalking solutions and developing problutions through problem finding can be divided into three major stages, plus an optional fourth stage: Sensing, Searching, Finding, and Transforming. These stages are described in Chapters Four through Eight using a hunting metaphor:

Mapping the Territory: Sensing Problutions (Sensing, Chapter Four), Preparing for the Chase: Redefinitional Techniques (Searching, Chapter Five), More Chase Preparations: Supplemental Redefinitional Techniques (Searching, Chapter Six), Flushing Out the Prey: Basic Strategies (Finding, Chapter Seven), and Transformations (Transforming, Chapter Eight). Although presented serially, there usually will be some overlap among these stages. This will be especially true when the larger problem situation contains many elements and is in a constant state of change.

The Sensing stage involves developing an increased awareness about your larger problem situation and your ability to deal with it. This awareness is achieved largely through the use of questions and sifting through all available information. The Searching stage requires you to use results from the previous stage and isolate major areas of difficulty in the general problem situation. The primary purpose of this stage is to gain a new perspective on your problem. If you haven't been successful to this point in the process, you can enter the Finding stage and analyze your problem situation in general. To do this, you will need to continue gathering relevant information and begin to flush out a well-defined problem statement. The last stage, Transforming, usually will be optional and reserved only for the most difficult-to-resolve situations. During this stage, you will need to conduct a detailed, specific problem analysis and hope a problution results.

At this point, your hunt should be over—at least as far as the general problem situation is concerned. New problems may become evident or new ones may be created during your hunt. You then will need to decide if you want to start stalking again.

It was a day like any other day in the big city. Mike Dallas eased himself behind the wheel of his battered sedan. Gunning the engine and pulling away from the curb, he confidently patted the left breast pocket of his suit to feel the secure outline of his .44 in its holster. He knew catching up with Bruno would not be easy. But, once he did, he needed to be prepared.

A dark shadow had settled over the city as night approached. Car lights bounced off buildings and other cars like a ball in a pinball machine. Commuters were making their way out of the city, while the night people began slinking in.

There were a million and one places for a man like Bruno to hide. And a million and one places for a man like Bruno to set up an ambush. Places where Mike might be expected to go to lose himself and his troubles after a hard day of sleuthing. He twitched in his seat as he thought of Bruno lurking about. He glanced into his rear-view mirror. The lights of the car behind him could be beams of death emanating from Bruno's eyes. They could be. Mike tugged on the borrowed clerical collar he wore and smiled smugly as he contemplated the night ahead. The stalking had begun.

She was a dame like any other dame. Except there was something different about her. Something about the way she walked; about the way she looked at you when you passed her on the street. Her long, auburn tresses cascaded down her back like rivulets of golden mountain water. And her eyes. Her eyes. They were the type of eyes that seemed to say everything, but said nothing at all. Eyes that almost seemed to swallow you when she looked at you. Yet, there also was a certain toughness about them. A toughness earned from years of hanging out with creeps like Bruno.

As his car idled at the traffic light, Mike Dallas noticed her strutting next to the curb, and reflected on other dames he has known. For some reason, they all seemed alike, yet they were all so different. There was just no figuring them out. Some were all over you and then, when you showed the least bit of interest, they were gone. Others played hard to get. And then, when you got 'em, you didn't want 'em any more. And then there was an even stranger type of dame . . . the type you could never figure out no matter how hard you tried.

Mike glanced to his right just as the light changed. She was gone, blended in with a thousand other prowling night faces. She probably knew where Bruno was, but she wasn't going to talk to Mike now—at least not yet.

As he eased his battered sedan into third gear, he knew how he could get to Bruno before Bruno got him. Bruno's girl, Mitzi, would lead Mike right to him. Mitzi of the auburn hair and warm eyes. But he hoped she didn't make any wrong moves. There wasn't much time.

Just as there are many different types of "dames," there also are many different types of problem-solving models. Most of these models are organized into a series of stages, with some including a provision for various types of feedback loops. The stages typically include such activities as: diagnose the problem, generate ideas, select the best idea, implement the idea selected, and evaluate the effectiveness of the implemented idea.

Although problem diagnosis usually is given at least "lip service" in these models, much more attention usually is paid to idea generation or one of the other stages. Most people seem to have a natural tendency to gloss over problem analysis in favor of idea generation. They seem to be afflicted with a severe case of "Assume-I-Knowitis." That is, they assume they (or anyone else affected by the problem) know what the problem is. Unfortunately, few efforts generally are made to test these assumptions.

Assume-I-Knowitis can be observed in many group meetings. A group will spend some time throwing out possible solutions to a problem that was vaguely stated at the outset. Finally, after seeming to run around in circles for hours, someone will ask: "Now, just what was our problem?" Because no effort was made to attempt understanding the problem situation, the group operated under a norm of implicit problem understanding. Had the group developed an explicit understanding of the problem instead, the members could have saved themselves considerable time and frustration. Moreover, a high quality solution might have been more likely.

There are several problem-solving approaches which emphasize the importance of spending time on problem analysis. All these approaches devote at least one stage to gathering problem information or ensuring that the "right" problem is found. Understanding how these approaches deal with problem finding can provide useful background information for understanding and assessing the stalking approach described in this book.

Four of these approaches will be discussed in this chapter: (1) Creative Problem-Solving (Parnes, Noller & Biondi, 1977), (2) Kepner-Tregoe (Kepner & Tregoe, 1981), (3) Lateral Thinking (de Bono, 1970), and (4) Synectics (Gordon, 1961). With the exception of the

Kepner-Tregoe (K-T) approach, all are designed primarily for dealing with ill-structured types of problems. That is, they will be useful for attempting to resolve problems that are not clearly defined and which require divergent thinking to generate solutions (although convergent thinking also plays a role in these approaches). The K-T approach, in contrast, is designed more for dealing with analytical, convergent types of problems for which there is one correct solution.

Creative Problem Solving

Creative Problem Solving (CPS) uses a five-step model for dealing with ill-structured types of problems: (1) Fact-Finding, (2) Problem-Finding, (3) Idea-Finding, (4) Solution-Finding, and (5) Acceptance-Finding. The guiding principle within all of these stages is deferred judgment.

In using this model, problem solvers are confronted with an ambiguous mess or challenge that seldom is clearly understood or defined. To help clarify this situation, problem solvers begin by using Fact-Finding to gather relevant information. When all relevant information has been collected, the Problem-Finding stage begins. In this stage, the collected information is reviewed and a variety of problem statements are developed. After additional analysis, one is selected and used to begin the third stage, Idea-Finding. In this stage, ideas are generated using a variety of techniques. The number of ideas is narrowed down and the final candidates are used to begin the Solution-Finding stage. During Solution-Finding, the remaining ideas are evaluated against weighted criteria and a final solution is selected. This solution is prepared for acceptance (if needed) and implemented during the last stage, Acceptance-Finding.

As can be seen in **Figure 2-1**, each major stage of the CPS process involves both convergent and divergent activities. Fact-Finding begins with a divergent search

Figure 2-1. The five-step CPS process.

Note: FF = Fact-Finding; PF = Problem-Finding; IF = Idea-Finding; SF = Solution-Finding; AF = Acceptance-Finding

for facts and then a covergent narrowing down of the facts to a more clearly-defined general area. In Problem-Finding, alternative problem definitions are generated (divergence), followed by the selection (convergence) of a definition which seems to capture best the problem question of concern to the problem solver. Idea-Finding begins with a divergent search for potential ideas followed by a convergent reduction of the total number of ideas. Solution-Finding involves two phases of divergence and convergence: (1) criteria are generated and then reduced in number, and (2) the ideas are modified (if needed) and a tentative solution is selected. In the last stage, Acceptance-Finding, ways are generated (divergence) to gain acceptance for the solution and its implementation. Selection of acceptance and implementation plans constitutes the convergence phase of Acceptance-Finding.

Although the five-step CPS process normally is described as a linear set of activities involving separate activities within each stage, it actually is more nonlinear and recursive. And, the activities within each stage are rarely mutually exclusive. That is, what is done within one stage more than likely will have an effect upon the other four stages. This interdependence of the stages is especially true for Fact-Finding, Problem-Finding, and Idea-Finding. These stages serve primarily to clarify and structure the original problem mess so a workable solution can emerge. Solution-Finding is, essentially, a decision-making stage and Acceptance-Finding is concerned with getting the solution applied to the problem. Thus, the first three stages are more interdependent than the last two.

It could be argued that problem finding within the CPS process is really a matter of progressing through the first three stages. Although one stage has been labeled as Problem-Finding, the net result of all three stages is a found problem (or, at least, it is hoped that is the net result). The problem cannot be "found" until information about the general problem mess first has been gathered (Fact-Finding). This information then is organized and synthesized to produce alternative problem definitions, any one of which may have the potential to resolve the original problem mess (Problem-Finding). The role of Idea-Finding in all of this might be viewed as further clarification of the mess, as symbolized by the use of one problem definition selected during the Problem-Finding stage. (Further extending this logic, it also could be argued that Solution-Finding is involved in the general process of problem finding, since the final decision of which solution to apply to the problem is made during this stage.)

Although this view of problem finding within the CPS process may be debatable, it must be acknowledged that the Problem-Finding stage does not exist in isolation. With this in mind, the Problem-Finding stage will be discussed in a little more detail to help understand how it contributes to dealing with the original problem mess.

As described by Parnes, Noller, and Biondi (1977), Biondi (1972), and Noller (1977), Problem-Finding has the objective of developing a problem statement that will permit optimal idea stimulation. That is, the mess should be described so that an almost unlimited number of ideas will seem possible for resolving the mess. Although there are no rigid guidelines or required techniques for Problem-Finding, there are certain activities that, if followed, will be more likely to lead to a problem redefinition that captures the "essence" of the problem mess.

The Problem-Finding stage usually begins by examining all the relevant information generated during Fact-Finding. Problem solvers then are instructed to write down a statement which captures the problem, using the format: "In What Ways Might I (IWWMI) . . . ?" For example, if the general problem situation concerns job dissatisfaction, the problem solver might rephrase this as: "IWWMI learn new job skills?" Many other redefinitions should be developed and, in all cases, judgment should be withheld. The objective is to generate as many redefinitions as possible so that the "right" problem (for the problem solver) will have an opportunity to emerge. If each redefinition is examined with an overly-critical eye, the "right" problem is not likely to present itself. Generating these redefinitions can involve using one of the techniques described next or by simply recording random redefinitions that might "pop up" during the Problem-Finding stage.

The next activity during Problem-Finding is to apply the "Why" technique to broaden the original definition. This technique involves asking why you believe a redefinition represents your problem and then writing down an answer. This answer is then used as another redefinition which you also should question, using the "Why" procedure.

As a simple illustration, consider the problem of learning new job skills. In this situation, the problem solver might ask: "Why" do I want to learn new job skills?" This question might be answered by responding with: "To have more variety in my job." Then, this answer would be reworded as: "IWWMI have more variety in my job?" and answered with: "Why do I want to have more variety in my job?" This process would continue until the redefinitions become so abstract that they are meaningless

(or unsolvable), or until the problem solver becomes aware of a potential solution through the broadening actions of the "Why" technique. If an obvious solution has not presented itself at this point, another problem statement can be selected and the process repeated.

Another way to capture the essence of problem statements is to change the subjects or verbs in the statement and make them more general. For instance, a problem involving ways to design a new telephone might be reworded in terms of ways people might communicate with one another electronically. Such a restatement would open up an entirely new direction for Idea-Finding. However, it still would have to be compatible with the objectives and resources of the problem solver. A telephone manufacturer, for example, might be restricted to telephone variations.

Problem-Finding also is concerned with identifying subproblems. Most complex problems cannot be dealt with in one fell swoop. Nor are they so simple that a single-track approach will alleviate the situation. Instead, many ill-structured problems require that they be broken down into subproblems with each subproblem dealt with separately. For instance, the previous problem of ways to increase job variety might be broken down into subproblems of variety in relation to other workers, in quantitative tasks, and in ways information is sent and received.

The final Problem-Finding activity involves reviewing all the problem redefinitions and selecting one that best describes the challenge the problem solver wants to meet. This, of course, will be a subjective activity. However, it is important to choose the redefinition that "feels right," which represents the problem the problem solver most needs to solve at this time. Once this is done, the problem solver can move to Idea-Finding. However, any time new information is acquired, the problem solver should feel free to develop a new redefinition and proceed from there.

Kepner-Tregoe

Charles Kepner and Benjamin Tregoe (1981), the originators of the Kepner-Tregoe (K-T) approach, believe that "rational processes" is a more appropriate name than problem solving for the thinking activities managers use to handle problems and decisions. Their four-stage model of "rational management" has gained considerable popularity around the world and has been used widely in a variety of organizations. The four stages of their model—Situation Appraisal, Problem Analysis, Decision Analysis, and Potential Problem Analysis—are viewed as reflecting four kinds of questions managers ask every day: (1) What's going on?, (2) Why did this happen?, (3) Which course of action should we take?, and (4) What lies ahead?

Situation Appraisal is used to evaluate a problem situation and determine the most appropriate analytical technique to use. Problem Analysis is used whenever it is determined that there is a deviation between expected and actual performance. Problem Analysis can help uncover the cause of this deviation. Decision Analysis involves choice situations in which objectives need to be established to engage in some activity. Finally, Potential Problem Analysis is used whenever the need exists to avoid future trouble when implementing a decision. Depending upon the results of the Situation Appraisal, the analytical techniques may be used in their entirety or only partially. Moreover, all or none of the analytical techniques may be needed for any given problem situation.

The Situation Appraisal process begins with a recognition of concerns that require action and for which you have some degree of responsibility. This can be ac-

complished by: (1) listing current deviations, threats, and opportunities; (2) examining current progress against goals; (3) trying to anticipate surprises in the future; or (4) searching for ways to improve current situations. The second major appraisal activity involves separating concerns into manageable components. Complex situations frequently require that information be gathered to determine if more than two components might exist. The third step is to set priorities to assess the order in which the components should receive attention. Determination of these priorities is based upon three criteria: (1) seriousness of the concern, (2) the amount of time urgency, and (3) the best estimate of probable growth of the concern. The last Situation Appraisal activity deals with planning for resolution of the concerns. This is accomplished by deciding how much of each of the three analytical processes (Problem Analysis, Decision Analysis, Potential Problem Analysis) will be required to resolve the concerns. In some cases, all of a process may be used, while in other cases only a partial process may be required.

Problem Analysis is selected if there is a need to determine why a concern happened. The first activity is to define the problem in terms of a deviation from an expected standard of performance. The second is to describe the problem by specifying its four major dimensions of: (1) identity (what is being explained), (2) location (where it is observed), (3) timing (when it occurs), and (4) magnitude (how serious and extensive it is). Then, each specification is described in terms of what is and what is not. The third Problem Anaylsis stage involves pulling out key information in the four dimensions of the problem and generating possible causes. The two major activities here are to determine what distinctions exist among the four dimensions describing identity, timing, location, and magnitude of the problem and changes that may exist among the distinctions that might suggest a problem cause. Testing for the most probable cause is the fourth stage of the process. Each possible cause is examined intensively against the specifications to try to explain what is and what is not likely as a cause. Finally, the last stage of this process involves verifying the actual cause of the problem.

Decision Analysis is the third rational thinking process used in the K-T approach. This process begins with a decision statement which includes information about the purpose and organizational level of the decision analysis. Next, objectives are developed in the form of "musts" and "wants." In the third stage, the objectives are assigned relative weights. The fourth stage involves generating a set of alternatives capable of meeting the objectives. Finally, in the fifth stage, each alternative is evaluated against the "musts" and "wants" and weighted numerically on a ten-point scale. The last activity during this stage is to examine possible adverse consequences of each alternative.

Potential Problem Analysis (PPA) is concerned with future events and their consequences. Although used less frequently than the other rational processes, Kepner and Tregoe believe that PPA is necessary to help protect decisions from adverse consequences. The first PPA activity is to identify the general problems of a project by looking for vulnerable areas. The second activity is to identify specific potential problems. This activity can be facilitated by specifying the what, where, when, and extent of each thing likely to go wrong within an area of vulnerability. The third major activity involves identifying likely causes and preventive actions. The fourth and final activity is to identify contingency plans for actions which might not be prevented.

These four processes of the K-T approach parallel some of the activities of the five-step Osborn-Parnes CPS model. Fact-Finding and Problem-Finding in the CPS model seem roughly analogous to Situation Appraisal and Problem Analysis in the K-T process. Idea-Finding and Solution-Finding roughly approximate some of the activities of Decision Analysis, and Acceptance-Finding seems to be similar to portions of Potential Problem Analysis. However, there are several noteworthy differences.

First, Situation Appraisal provides explicit criteria to use in deciding which of the other problem-solving activities will be needed. Second, the K-T approach seems to ignore any systematic attempts at generating ideas. The use of creative problem-solving techniques does not seem to have a place in "rational" thinking. Finally, the Situation Appraisal and Problem Analysis processes seem to be most involved in the general problem-finding process. Situation Appraisal, in particular, seems to provide somewhat of a structured approach for determining how to deal with a problem situation.

It must be noted that Situation Appraisal may be too structured for adequately analyzing ill-structured types of problems. The overall format of the Fact-Finding and Problem-Finding stages of the CPS model seem to be more flexible and adequate to the task of working with ill-structured problems. However, it may be that there are several features of Situation Appraisal that might be adopted for use in the CPS process.

Lateral Thinking

Edward de Bono (1970) developed Lateral Thinking as a way to counteract the dysfunctional thinking patterns which often inhibit people from developing creative solutions to their problems. Lateral Thinking attempts to disrupt these patterns by creating awareness of the mind's patterning system, exploring differences between vertical and lateral thinking, and applying special techniques. The special techniques have operational relevance to problem finding and will be discussed next.

According to de Bono, special techniques involve three sets of activities: awareness, alternatives, and

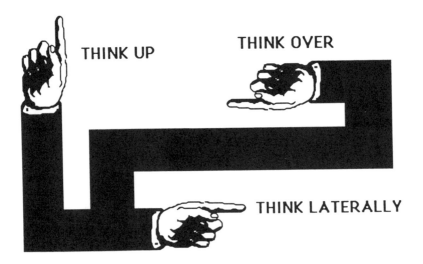

provocative methods. Awareness activities are used to redefine and clarify current ideas. Among the techniques for doing this are: dominant ideas, tethering factors, polarizing tendencies, boundaries, and assumptions. The use of alternatives involves trying to develop a variety of problem perspectives. No one perspective is viewed as "correct," since the objective is simply to break away from old ways of looking at the problem. Alternatives used by de Bono include: rotation of attention, change of entry point, quota of alternatives, concept changing, fractionation, and bridging divisions. The third set of activities, provocative methods, is designed to help generate new ideas. These methods include such techniques as: reversal, distortion and exaggeration, exposure, cross-fertilization, problem switching, analogies, and random-word stimulation.

Awareness activities appear to be useful because of their emphasis upon understanding current problem perceptions. Being aware of dominant ideas can help maintain an open mind in viewing the overall problem situation during different stages of analysis. Identifying tethering factors can help avoid making unwarranted assumptions about a problem. According to de Bono, tethering factors are overlooked aspects of problems that can restrict the range of possible solutions. De Bono uses the example of a problem involving reducing the number of commuter cars to make more room for shoppers. If the tethering factor is that parking rates will be lower the longer a car is parked, a creative solution may be blocked. However, if parking rates increase over time, a creative solution may be achieved since commuters would be less likely to park in such locations. A third awareness activity is polarizing tendencies, or the tendency of a problem to contain an either-or type of situation. For instance, external constraints may limit the number of ways a problem can be viewed, as in the case of environmentalists and energy producers. Boundaries represent the "space" available for problem solving as perceived by the problem solver. Past experience often places limits on our ability to view a problem in many different ways. Assumptions, the last awareness activity discussed by de Bono, deals with the need to recognize that we all make certain assumptions about all problems. To develop unique problem perspectives, we should be aware of as many assumptions as possible for each problem situation.

While awareness activities can be useful in understanding current problem perceptions, alternatives help in breaking away from old ways of viewing a problem. Avoidance devices can help us escape from nonproductive assumptions and perceptions. Rotation of attention involves shifting focus from one part of a problem to another. For example, no-fault insurance shifts attention from an insurance company's claims procedures to customer benefits and satisfaction. Change of entry point concerns the usefulness of using a nonconventional way to analyze a problem. An example would be a problem of reducing traffic congestion in a particular area by starting from the points at which cars enter and leave the area. Quota of alternatives is used to help motivate problem solvers to generate many different ways of viewing a problem. The important point is not to generate many "correct" viewpoints, but many different viewpoints. Concept changing attempts to avoid a fixed problem perspective by stating the problem differently. For instance, a problem of parking cars might be restated in terms of ways to store things. Fractionation, a fifth alternatives activity, involves dividing a problem into different parts without regard to the correctness of the division. Finally, bridging divisions try to provide new perspectives by combining two apparently unrelated concepts.

Provocative methods are specifically designed to help develop new ideas by altering problem perspectives.

Reversals change the direction of a problem statement. For example, instead of looking for ways to reduce traffic congestion, the problem solver might think in terms of ways to increase congestion. Although such a change might not appear to be logical, it should provide a new perspective. Distortion and exaggeration serve the same purpose by changing part of a situation or taking it to an extreme (e.g., cars moving at the speed of light). Exposure involves using things unrelated to the problem as stimuli for ideas. Cross-fertilization, a fourth provocative method, generates ideas by obtaining the perspectives of people from fields unrelated to the problem area. Problem switching is used by stopping work on one problem and switching to another. Presumably, when the original problem is attacked again, new perspectives will have been gained. Analogies generate ideas and new problem perspectives by considering what else is similar to the problem and using these similarities as stimuli. The last provocative method used by de Bono is random-word stimulation. It involves randomly selecting words from a dictionary (or other word source) and using the words as stimuli, even though they may be unrelated to the problem.

In contrast to the CPS approach and the Kepner-Tregoe method, Lateral Thinking is not so much a problem-solving model as it is a way of thinking about problems. As a result, it may be difficult for some to apply the methods described. However, the three major activities described by de Bono seem to be useful for developing unique problem perspectives and breaking away from the constraints we often place upon ourselves and our problem situations. As a result, we will be more likely to develop the "right" way of viewing our problems if we first avoid any notion of what is the "correct" problem perception. Lateral Thinking appears to be well-suited for this purpose.

Synectics

The Synectics approach to creative problem solving was developed by William Gordon (1961) and George Prince (1970). Synectics (which means the joining together of apparently irrelevant elements) relies upon analogies and metaphors to define problems and generate solutions.

Two important mechanisms of Synectics are making the strange familiar and making the familiar strange. Making the strange familiar is used to help develop a better understanding of the problem; making the familiar

SYNECTICS: "The joining together of two apparently unrelated elements."

MONA CLOWN

strange is designed to produce new problem perspectives so unique solutions can be achieved. Both mechanisms can be aided by using one or more different types of analogies: personal (personal identification with a problem), direct (parallel relationships with other objects or ideas), symbolic (use of objective and impersonal images), and fantasy (use of wish fulfillment) (Gordon, 1961).

A typical listing would include:

1. Describe the problem as given (PAG).
2. Using analogies, conduct a short analysis of the PAG to make the strange familiar.
3. Purge. Think of known or trivial solutions to the problem.
4. Using fantasy analogies, develop a problem as understood (PAU) by selecting a portion of the problem to work on.
5. Excursion. Develop analogies to the problem to help make the familiar strange and produce new problem perspectives.
6. Develop a fantasy force fit by examining the relationship between the analogy used in the excursion and the PAU.
7. Using the fantasy force fit, attempt to think of a practical solution to the problem (Practical Force Fit—PFF).
8. Examine the new viewpoint of the problem. If you consider the solution workable, terminate the process. However, if you don't consider the solution to be practical, use the viewpoint as a redefinition of the original problem and repeat the process.

Prince (1975) has re-assessed the thinking processes involved in Synectics and proposed the "Mindspring" theory as a different way to view the creative problem-solving process. Mindspring theory is based upon the use of six major thinking elements: wish, retrieve, compare, transform, store, and image. According to Prince, their effectiveness will depend upon the ability of the problem solver to alternate between a "tolerance for approximation and a wish for precision." As an example, Prince discusses a problem of developing a new type of closure for a thermos bottle. A problem solver typically might think of other types of closures, such as the slide on a spice can. In this case, the operation of the slide may suggest only an approximate solution. However, several modification attempts may lead to a more precise solution capable of solving the problem.

Continuing with the spice can example, Prince notes that wishing for a new type of closure for a thermos bottle would be a wish activity. It might then be followed by a retrieval of information, such as noting that a spice can has a unique type of closure. However, comparison with the thermos bottle indicates that the solution cannot be precisely like the spice can slide (a comparison activity). As a result, the problem solver may need to modify the size of the slide and the type of material used to satisfy the requirements of a thermos bottle (a transformation activity).

The next activity involves storing the solution just developed for future reference. Finally, Prince notes that the image activity probably was used at every step during the process as the problewm solver imaged what was mentally taking place. This illustration demonstrates that very few successful solutions are fully developed at the outset, but emerge only when the problem solver is able to tolerate approximate thinking.

In reviewing the eight-step Synectics process, it should be apparent that most stages are concerned with problem finding, either directly or indirectly. This is especially true of the processes of making the strange familiar and making the familiar strange. Both activities involve developing different problem perspectives.

Although all six elements of Mindspring theory seem to have some relevance to problem finding, wishing seems to be especially useful. This is probably because wishing is a basic mechanism for formulating problem definitions. Wishes can help enrich thinking about a problem and facilitate retrieval of relevant information (Prince, 1970). In fact, wishing could be one way to overcome the difficulty noted in some problem-solving research of accessing previously-acquired information (e.g., Perfetto, Bransford & Franks, 1983).

However, the major relevance of Mindspring theory seems to lie with the process of approximate thinking. By structuring the process to include tolerance of approximate retrievals and ways of looking at a problem and solutions, the problem solver will be more likely to find the "right" problem. That is, it will be easier for the problem solver to successively transform the original problem situation into a desired problem state. In sum, Mindspring theory seems to do an excellent job of capturing the problem finding process.

His bed seemed especially hard for some reason. Hard, like concrete is hard. And the sparks in front of his eyes darted about like sparks from a subway train rounding a corner. Shaking his head and looking about, Mike finally figured out why his bed felt so hard. Concrete. He had been lying on concrete. The hard type of concrete. And the sparks in front of his eyes weren't sparks from a subway train, although his head felt as if he had been hit by one.

Easing himself up from his concrete bed, Mike's head gradually began to clear. The alley he found himself in was behind Mitzi's apartment. When he followed her home, he forgot one important rule of detective work: Never get too close to your prey. You might be spotted and lose it.

However, Mitzi never did recognize Mike in his clerical garb, stalking along behind her. But Bruno did. Waiting in his car in front of his girlfriend's apartment, Bruno spotted Mitzi being followed. He knew it could be only one person. It then was just a simple matter of sneaking up on our detective hero and hitting him on the head with a tire iron. Iron and bone can make sparks when just the right amount of force is applied. And sparks were all Mike saw for over three and one-half hours.

Mike now knew that he was going about things all wrong. Bruno was a lot smarter than he thought. If Bruno had wanted to, he easily could have disposed of Mike permanently. He must be up to something. But a detective's instincts might not be adequate to the task that lay ahead. Mike now would have to become more analytical. He would need to learn more about Bruno and his "M.O." Sure, Bruno was cruel and devious. But so were a million other hoodlums in the big city. There must be something to distinguish Bruno from all the other hoods. All Mike had to do was find it.

Pulling up his coat collar to shut out a sudden gust of cold air, Mike knew that he now would have to play by Bruno's rules. He would have to learn what Bruno ate, what he did during the day, and who he did it with. In short, Mike needed to know Bruno as well as one person could know another . . . even if that person was someone you despised . . . and even if that person was someone capable of snuffing out your life in an instant!

CHAPTER THREE

IDENTIFYING THE PREY:
RECOGNIZING PROBLUTIONS

After donating his now useless clerical garb to the Salvation Army, Mike drove at a slow, but steady pace down Blaine Street. He needed time to think. Bruno was not fooled by his ruse and Mike seemed to be having trouble tracking him down. Collecting more information about him might be the answer, if he knew where to look. Or with whom he should talk.

Just after braking for a youthful-looking bag lady, Mike remembered Purvis O'Donnell or PO as he was known to his fellow street people. PO always seemed to know everything about the local hoods. Whenever he sought out PO, Mike usually came away with vital information for a case—information that added a new perspective.

PO never seemed to live any place in particular. Today, Mike found him on a side street just off of Blaine. When Mike pulled up to the curb, PO was pacing back and forth in front of a newsstand.

"What's buggin' ya, PO? You look like you're a little steamed."

"Yeah? Well, I am!" snorted PO. "I was just ripped off by a bag lady. Took every penny I had saved up for my ma's gall bladder operation!"

"Tough luck, Buddy, but I need some information. If you can help me, I'll give ya my gall bladder."

Never one to turn down an act of charity, PO consented to help Mike. When Mike asked him what he knew about Bruno, PO's eyes lit up like a kid with his first girlie magazine. PO had seen Bruno a week ago. He had been running out of one of those little specialty stores that sold over-priced chocolate. The proprietor was running after him shouting "Stop, thief!" Later, PO learned that Bruno had not stolen any money. Fifty pounds of chocolate was all he took.

Mike rubbed his chin and looked up toward the concrete and steel obelisks rising out of the cement fields. So, Bruno was addicted to chocolate—a bona fide chocoholic. Now he knew just what type of fiend he was dealing with. A fiend who would stop at nothing to get a fix of the brown elixir!

Mike believes that he has now obtained some useful information. He now knows about Bruno's craving for chocolate. However, this may not be enough information. It also may not be useful for what he needs to continue his pursuit of Bruno. Nevertheless, Mike has structured the situation so he at least has a slightly better understanding of Bruno.

From these developments, it could be said that the rules of the game have changed somewhat. Mike no longer has to search randomly for Bruno. He now can afford to be a bit more systematic. The rules still are likely to change, but Mike expects that to happen.

The situation is somewhat like Chinese baseball (also identified by others as Egyptian football). As soon as the ball is thrown, the players are free to change the rules in any way they see fit. However, the more a group of individuals play together, the more likely it is that a set of rules will emerge that are understood (if not followed) by all involved. It is this ability to seek and achieve understanding of a situation that forms the basis for most problem-finding activities.

Many approaches to problem finding have their roots in the work of the Gestaltists (e.g., Duncker, 1945; Wertheimer, 1959). They emphasized the achievement of understanding during problem solving—the grasping of the "essence" of a situation. Therefore, the way to solve problems is to seek understanding of them.

Unfortunately, we do not always have the time to understand our problems fully. Instead, we make snap judgments about what our problems are. When presented with ill-structured problems (ISPs), we often rapidly transform them into well-structured problems (WSPs) so we can begin to deal with them. Sometimes this works and sometimes it does not. Rapid transformations work when our understanding of the situation is adequate for resolving the situation. However, they are likely to fail when understanding is based upon erroneous perceptions about the larger problem situation.

Making snap judgments about problem situations is not necessarily "bad". We all tend to evaluate new information when we first encounter it. The important thing is that we tend to evaluate this new information in light of what we already know about similar situations (Glaser, 1984). This is what provides structure to often poorly-defined situations. However, we sometimes make poor assessments and correctly interpret the "wrong" situation in light of a previous situation or incorrectly interpret the "right" situation. In either case, eventual resolution of the situation is likely to be delayed.

Whenever we evaluate problem situations and add structure to them we are using a rough form of problem finding. Every time we identify a situation as possessing a particular set of elements, we have classified that situation in the context of previous perceptions. Thus, our search for understanding is based upon a typology of problems we all develop. This typology may not be the same for everyone, but everyone needs one to solve problems.

Importance of Problem Types

Since it will be much easier to discuss problem types with a common frame of reference, a problem typology will be presented and discussed in this chapter. Such a typology is important because of its ability to provide a common framework for communicating about widely-divergent types of problems. However, problem typologies also have other advantages.

First, typologies can provide the primary basis for dealing with most ISPs. Our reactions to most problem situations usually are affected by our initial perceptions. If these are invalid, resolution will be more difficult. On the other hand, use of a typology can help structure and understand problems. As a result, typologies can help eliminate the tendency to place too much emphasis upon initial reactions.

Second, a common typology can help us avoid becoming "locked in" to a particular view of a problem. That is, it can help eliminate the possibility of developing personalized stereotypes to our problems. A typology can do this by providing a more or less systematic way to break down problems into their major parts. If every problem is reduced in a similar manner, personalized stereotyping will be less likely to occur.

Finally, a common typology helps us appreciate the variety and complexity of most problems. We often tend to categorize problems in ways in which we are not always aware. Such behavior can make it difficult to appreciate the diversity of problems we often face.

Before looking at the typology used in this book, a word of caution is necessary. No typology can be all-encompassing (Reitman, 1965). Trying to develop such a typology would be foolish. Any framework that begins to approach the realities and complexities of real-life problems would drown in its own variables and relationships. Thus, the typology presented next must, of necessity, be simplified.

A Typology of Problems

Most problems can be classified as either well-structured (WSPs) or ill-structured (ISPs), with many variations in between. The difference between a WSP and an ISP is determined by a problem's three major components. According to Reitman (1964; 1965) and others (e.g., MacCrimmon & Taylor, 1976; Simon, 1973), these components are: (1) an initial state, (2) a goal state, and (3) some means of transforming the initial state into the goal state.

The constraints of a WSP are closed at the outset. Problem solvers usually can solve such problems as formulated. That is, the transformations needed to close the gap between the initial and goal states are clear-cut. In contrast, the constraints of an ISP usually are more open at the outset and much less clear-cut. However, as the problem solver adds structure to the problem, the constraints become much less open until the problem is solved.

Although some problems may be "pure" WSPs or "pure" ISPS, this rarely will be the case. Most problem situations present themselves as being somewhere between the two extremes represented by WSPs and ISPs. When different situations are viewed as possessing different degrees of structure, a variety of problem types can be described.

Reitman (1964; 1965), for example, describes the classical problem of converting a sow's ear into a silk purse. In this case, the initial and goal states are fairly well known. The major task is one of discovering a way to transform the ear into a silk purse. As another example, Reitman borrows a situation described by Gordon (1961): Invent a dispenser which can be used with various products. The dispenser should be one piece, have a non-removable top, and a mouth that can be opened easily for dispensing and closed tightly after being used. With this type of problem, neither the initial nor the goal states are well-specified (although the goal state is more structured than the initial state). Thus, not much information is available about how to transform the initial state into the goal state.

Reitman also describes other types of problems, such as the one faced by Napoleon's chef after the defeat of the Austrians at the battle of Marengo. The chef was charged with creating a celebration dinner with a relatively limited variety of available ingredients: chicken,

mushrooms, onions, tomatoes, and wine. The result was Chicken Marengo. In this case, the chef was faced with a problem in which the initial state was specified clearly, but the goal state and the needed transformations were unclear. Altogether, Reitman discusses six different problem types, all of which vary according to how much is specified about the initial and goal states.

Taylor (1974) later expanded and elaborated upon Reitman's work. According to Taylor, the most important determinant of problem type is the degree of familiarity problem solvers have with each problem component. In solving a problem, we often perceive its components in light of previous problems we have tried to solve. We also might view a component as familiar based upon previous problem solving experience, educational experiences, or knowledge of available resources which might be used to resolve the problem (e.g., a program library). In any event, a problem will not be perceived by problem solvers as familiar unless it is seen as one that has been solved previously.

According to Taylor (1974), when the initial state is unfamiliar and the transformations and goal state vary (i.e., they are either familiar or unfamiliar), a resource specification problem exists. An example of this type of problem would be students who are unsure of their vocational capabilities. A goal specification problem exists when the goal state is unfamiliar and the initial state and transformations vary. An example would be a product improvement, such as ways to design a better toaster. When the transformations are unfamiliar and the initial and goal states vary, a creative problem exists. Developing a new type of fuel for automobiles would be an example of this type of problem. Finally, Taylor describes a type of problem in which problem solvers are familiar with the transformations and the initial and goal states. This type of problem is well-structured and can be solved by applying routine procedures.

Using these descriptions of problem types, Taylor suggests that problems can be reformulated by opening or closing constraints. Through the search for information, problem solvers can focus upon structuring the initial or goal states as well as the required transformations. The objective is to achieve a WSP in which a final solution is fairly obvious. As discussed in Chapter One, such a situation would be characteristic of a "problution".

Although Taylor's four-problem typology is useful, it is not developed fully, thereby limiting its practical value. In particular, several varieties of problem types are left undefined. By describing a problem's states as variable (either familiar or unfamiliar), the range of problem types is restricted. For example, Taylor describes a resource specification problem as one in which the initial state is unfamiliar and the goal state and transformations are either familiar or unfamiliar. Depending upon the familiarity of problem solvers with these states, a resource specification problem could be represented in one of four different ways. For instance, with an unfamiliar initial state, the problem also could have an unfamiliar goal state. In this case, the problem also could be classified as a goal specification problem.

To avoid this confusion and provide a more realistic way of classifying problems based upon familiarity, I have modified Taylor's classification scheme as shown in **Table 3-1.** The solid circles and completed rabbit figures represent closed constraints which, by definition, are problem components familiar to problem solvers. The unfilled circles and uncompleted rabbit figures represent open constraints and can be considered unfamiliar to problem solvers. By dichotomizing the three components according to their familiarity or unfamiliarity to the problem solver, eight problem types are created.

The first four problem types have initial states which are familiar to you. A type I problem is identical to the WSP described by Taylor—you are familiar with the initial and goal states and the transformations. A Type II problem (Pure Transformational) is characterized by familiarity with the initial and goal states, but relatively little is known about how to reduce the gap between these states. A Type III problem is described as a Pure Goal problem, since you are presumed to be familiar with all the problem components except the goal state. Type IV problems are situations where you are familiar with only the initial state. These problems are Transformational/Goal problems, since you need to structure the goals as well as to make the needed transformations.

The remaining four problem types are distinguished by initial states which are essentially unfamiliar to you. A Pure Resource problem is a Type V problem. When these situations are perceived, you are unfamiliar with only the initial state. Type VI problems (Resource/Transformational) require specification of initial states and transformations, since you are familiar only with the goal state. Resource/Goal problems (Type VII) are characterized by familiarity with transformations, but little

Table 3-1. Classification of problem types based upon familiarity.

PROBLEM COMPONENTS

PROBLEM TYPES	Initial	Goal	Transformations
I. Well-Structured	🐭	🐭	●
II. Pure Transformational	🐭	🐭	?
III. Pure Goal	🐭	☞	●
IV. Transformational/Goal	🐭	☞	?
V. Pure Resource	☞	🐭	●
VI. Resource/Transformational	☞	🐭	?
VII. Resource/Goal	☞	☞	●
VIII. Pure Ill-Structured	☞	☞	?

Note: 🐭 = Familiar with a problem component

☞ = Unfamiliar with a problem component

● = Familiar with a solution

? = Unfamiliar with a solution

knowledge or understanding about the initial and goal states. Such situations could be described as solutions in search of problems. Finally, Type VIII problems are Pure ISPs at the opposite end of the continuum from WSPs. When dealing with Pure ISPs, you have little or no familiarity with the states or the transformations involved.

During the creative problem-solving process, you typically will start with some form of an ISP. As you become more and more familiar with the problem by adding or clarifying information, your perception of the problem gradually will approach that of a "pure" WSP. However, at each step along the way, you will be faced with a different type of problem. Sometimes, you will perceive this problem as well-structured and sometimes as ill-structured. (According to Simon (1973), all problems are ISPs. WSPs are ISPs that have been formalized.)

Because problems change over time, it would be useful to have a way of identifying problem situations in terms of the eight problem types. Taylor (1974) developed a simple decision tree for identifying his four primary problem types using questions about the degree of familiarity with the problem components. However, a slightly more complex tree would be needed for the eight types shown in **Table 3-1**. Such a tree is presented in **Figure 3-1**.

As shown in **Figure 3-1**, you would start with decision point A and decide if you are familiar with the initial problem state. You then would proceed to decision point B where you would decide if you are familiar with the goal state of the problem situation. Finally, you would go to decision point C where you would decide if you are familiar with the transformations needed to resolve the problem. Depending upon how you answer question C, you can classify the problem as belonging to one of the eight different types.

To illustrate how you might use this decision tree to identify problem types, consider the following illustra-

Figure 3-1. Decision tree for identifying problem types.

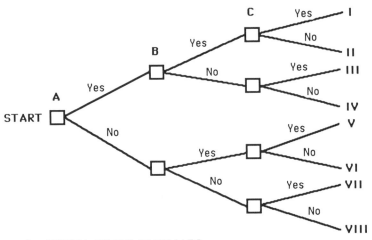

A: INITIAL STATE FAMILIAR?

B: TRANSFORMATION STATE FAMILIAR?

C. GOAL STATE FAMILIAR?

```
I    = Well-structured problem
II   = Goal problem
III  = Transformational problem
IV   = Transformational/goal problem
V    = Resource problem
VI   = Resource/goal problem
VII  = Resource/transformational problem
VIII = Ill-structured problem
```

tions. These examples are clearly simplified, since the decision tree uses only either-or responses and the situations described are hypothetical.

Suppose that you are a teacher interested in resolving the problem: IWWMI encourage students in my 1:10 p.m. class to stop making disruptive comments? For this problem, you might answer "yes" at decision point A, indicating that you are familiar with the problem. In this instance, you are fully aware of the existence of the disruptive comments. In response to question B, you might indicate that you are familiar with the goal state and respond with a "yes" (a lack of disruptive comments would be a typical preference for a goal in this situation). At upper level decision point C in **Figure 3-1**, you then might respond with a "no" to the question about your familiarity with the transformation state. You probably do not have many clear-cut, ready-made solutions available (although it would not be improbable to have a ready-made solution for this example). At this point, problem Type II would be identified—a Pure Transformational problem. Your task in this instance would be to develop ways of transforming the disruptive comments into a situation free from them.

As another illustration, suppose you are a business manager and one of your subordinates has been complaining to you about being dissatisfied with her job. Although a number of problem statements might be appropriate in this situation, you decide on the problem: IWWMI help my subordinate become more satisfied with her job? Beginning with decision point A, you might indicate that, "yes," you are familiar with the initial state. The employee is dissatisfied in terms of her descriptions of the situation. Next, you could respond to decision point B with a "no," since you are not clear about what it would take for this employee to be satisfied. Finally, you might answer decision point C with a "no," since you are uncertain at this time about any available solutions. This response

indicates that your initial perception of the problem would be a Type IV situation. This situation is known as a Transformational/Goal problem and implies that you will need to focus your initial efforts on defining the goal and then developing possible solutions.

To practice identifying the problem types, try the following hypothetical situation. You have been asked by your boss to develop a program to retrain workers whose jobs soon will be automated. You have known about the possibility of the automation for about six months, but your boss did not provide verification until almost three weeks before its expected occurrence. What type of problem situation are you facing?

Like most problem situations, this one is highly subjective. Your initial reactions and perceptions might determine the eventual classification of this problem. For example, you might decide that your problem is: IWWMI retrain workers who have just lost their jobs to automation? In this case, the sequence of your responses to the decision tree might be "yes," "no," and "no." This would be a Type IV problem as in the previous example. However, it also is possible that you might answer some of the same questions differently. For instance, you might decide initially that you are not very familiar with the retraining problem (and especially the need for it), that you are familiar with the goal, but you are not familiar with possible transformations. In this case, the situation would be a Type VI problem (Resource/Transformational) and require goal clarification and then development of alternative solutions.

Nature and Nuture of Problutions

Once you have identified the problem facing you, a solution should emerge after you have made the appropriate transformations. Making these transformations is the topic of the remaining chapters in this book. However, before looking at the processes involved in making transformations, it first will be helpful to understand more about the eight problem types and their relation to problutions. If you believe you understand problutions well enough to meet your needs, you might want to skip to the next chapter.

The problem-finding process is based upon the assumption that problems are perceived as ill-structured at the outset. Otherwise, there would be no need to proceed with structuring the problem situation. By adding additional information to the problem elements and evaluating how this information alters the relationship among the elements and your overall perception of the problem, a different view of the problem may emerge. When this view involves a perception that the problem constraints are closed, a problution probably exists and the problem situation may be considered resolved.

For instance, you might make $20,000 per year and wish to make $30,000 (a Type II problem). This situation is clearly ill-structured if you believe that there are many possible ways to close the constraints you perceive to exist. By devising different ways to transform your initial state into your goal state, you are problem solving in the sense that you are searching for a creative solution. That is, you are attempting to close the constraints using one or more actions. Thus, you might think of asking your boss for a $10,000 raise and then evaluate how likely it is that such an action would close the gap of your problem. In this case, you might decide that such an action is not likely to alter the relation between the problem states. No amount of pleading or persuasion may convince your boss that you are worth an extra ten grand.

Resigned to this realization, you then might decide to redefine your problem in terms of achieving greater job satisfaction. After generating and implementing several actions to increase your satisfaction, you no longer may feel the need to increase your salary. Instead you might decide to live with whatever problution you have created. You now have closed the constraints of your initial problem situation and see the situation as being well-structured rather than ill-structured. Of course, your perceptions might change at any time, and you then would have to engage in a new round of problem-finding.

The basic perceptual mechanism involved in the problem-finding process is pattern recognition. Every time you consider a problem, you will be thinking in terms of a new or previous set of problem elements organized in a particular way. The process of transforming them may result in a number of different patterns, depending upon how much information you have added at any particular time.

The act of recognizing an object involves similar operations. For example, when you are some distance from an object, you might see it as a vague set of patterns. It may be somewhat familiar to you in terms of its shape, color, texture, or other clues, but not enough to allow you to recognize it as an object with which you are familiar. However, as you move closer to it a new pattern may begin to form. You may begin to recognize familiar shapes or colors. Gradually, as you approach the object, the relations among the objects become clearer and assume greater meaning to you. Finally, at some point, everything falls into place and you experience full recognition. When this occurs, the feeling may be very similar to the "Aha!" experience that often accompanies what many (e.g., Wallas, 1926) refer to as sudden insight during creative problem solving.

Based upon Greeno's (1977) conceptualizations, the patterns which occur during problem finding can be classified as problem patterns and solution patterns. Problem patterns are the internal representations of a problem you develop during problem finding. That is, each time you perceive an ISP while attempting to develop a solution, you are dealing with a specific problem pattern. Solution patterns, in contrast, are more static and consist of the cognitive representations of a solved problem. They are the perceived relations among the initial problem

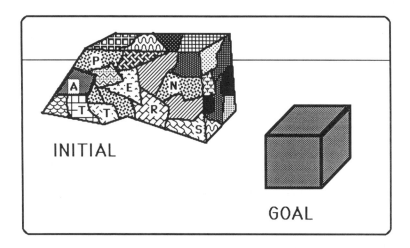

INITIAL

GOAL

elements and any new elements that may have been added while working with the problem patterns. Problem patterns occur during the problem-finding process, while solution patterns typically occur at the end of the problem-finding process.

Solution patterns are, in essence, problutions (although it also could be argued that problem patterns are solutions, depending upon the particular point in time the problem is being observed). Problutions are problem situations in which all necessary constraints have been closed and a solution is evident. You know you have produced a problution when you have sufficient understanding of the problem situation which is relevant to you. And, as noted previously, once you understand your problem, you have solved it.

It is this close relationship between problems and solutions that makes problem finding so important. Your solutions must be stalked *through* your problems. Even though they may be unknown to you at the outset, the solutions to your problems are a part of the problem situation you are trying to resolve. However, you first must "find" your problems during the stalking process. Once this is done, the solutions should be understood just as well as you understood your problems at the end of problem finding. At the risk of being redundant, to understand a problem is to understand its solution. In this regard, all creative problem-solving processes are attempts to facilitate and guide the problem finding process.

The extent to which you will be able to understand a problem situation will depend upon the situation. That is, some problems will be more difficult to understand than others. The particular degree of understanding you can achieve in working toward a problution will be determined by the criteria of coherence, correspondence, and "connectedness."

According to Greeno (1977) coherence refers to the extent that a problem is represented using the right type of information. Quality of information is more important than quantity, since the amount of information will not necessarily increase understanding. If the information you have about a problem seems to "hang together" in an integrated way, your problem is represented coherently to you. As a result, you probably have some degree of problem understanding.

Correspondence is the degree of relationship existing between the perceived problem and the "actual" problem. Making unwarranted assumptions about a problem and drawing incorrect conclusions would indicate a low degree of correspondence. For example, you might decide that your problem is developing ways to pay workers more money so they will be more productive. The workers, however, may be reducing their productivity in response to some new policy which they view as being unfair. For this situation to have high correspondence, you might have to focus your efforts upon dealing with the workers' attitudes, rather than their behavior.

The third criterion of understanding is connectedness. You will be more likely to understand a problem if you can relate other knowledge you possess to the problem situation. Thus, people with broad, general knowledge probably will exhibit greater connectedness with a variety of problems than persons with more specialized knowledge. In any event, your understanding of any problem situation will be enhanced if you can apply other relevant knowledge to it.

If you rate a problem situation as high in all three of these criteria, a problution should exist. That is, if your information about the problem seems to be internally consistent and well integrated (coherence), if you are dealing with the "right" problem for your situation and needs (correspondence), and if you are able to relate knowledge you possess to the problem (connectedness), then you should understand the problem well. However, if you rate your problem as being low on any one of these criteria, then your understanding would be diminished accordingly. You would be that much farther away from developing a problution.

It also should be noted that these three criteria could be used as rough guides to estimate how familiar you are with the components of a problem. In particular, the criteria should be especially useful for estimating familiarity with the initial and goal states and any relationships between them. For example, you might have the "right" information (coherence) about an initial state, but have totally inaccurate or misleading information (from your perspective) about the goal state. Thus, you might understand completely the difficulty you are having in dealing with some job-related tasks, but be totally in the dark about how you want to improve things. You might lack only the right kind of information needed to clarify a more desirable situation. Similar situations also might exist for the other two criteria.

Staking out chocolate stores was not Mike's idea of having fun. Making a big collar after a high-speed car chase was fun. Blasting a 20-point moose between the eyes was fun. Or, spending a night with the boys chugalugging until everyone was completely wasted—and then sick, was fun. Keeping an eye out for creeps like Bruno was hard work. Diverting your eyes for even less than a minute could cause you to lose your prey.

Mike had to keep reminding himself how badly he wanted to catch Bruno. Every time his eyes and thoughts began to wander, Mike tried to jolt himself back to reality by thinking of Bruno's arrogant attitude in his office. And how Bruno had given him a grapefruit-size knot on the back of his head when he found himself lying in the alley.

But none of these things really seemed important now. What really motivated Mike was PO. The little fellow was always ready to help. Just as long as Mike showed him the right color money. However, Mike had just found out that money wouldn't do PO any good any more. Not unless the street people in the sky had a use for it. Bruno apparently had recognized PO slinking among the other street people, stalked him for three blocks, and then slid a shiv into the lumbar region of his back. PO was no more.

Mike shook his head from side-to-side to clear the cobwebs. He thought he saw someone suspicious coming out of the chocolate store. Someone about Bruno's build and height wearing a long, gray trenchcoat and carrying a white sack weighted down with what could be only the brown elixir of the gods.

Mike felt his pulse race and his face flush. Should he leap out of his car and confront Bruno? Or, should he try to follow Bruno and see where he goes? The hunter hunting the hunted. He had to decide quickly. Darkness was beginning to fall and a night stalk would be extremely risky.

Bruno made a decision for Mike. He jumped in his car and sped directly toward Mike and his car. Peering over his steering wheel, Mike thought he detected a maniacal smile on Bruno's face. Or maybe it was just chocolate residue. No matter. Now was the time to act!

THE HUNT

CHAPTER FOUR

MAPPING THE TERRITORY

SENSING PROBLUTIONS

Gaining hold of his senses, Mike gunned his motor, slammed his car into reverse, and skillfully guided it out of his parking place and backward down the street. As he was doing this, Bruno sped toward Mike, his eyes transfixed. With his senses dulled by perhaps too much chocolate, Bruno's car missed Mike's by at least 20 feet. Instead of smashing broadside into his enemy's car, Bruno found his car rather neatly wrapped around a light pole and being ticketed by a meter maid for improper parking.

Mike wasn't able to observe all of this. He had his own problems in trying to weave his way backwards down the busy downtown street, all the while trying to maneuver around cars and pedestrians. However, as soon as he saw Bruno's car crash into the light pole, he jammed on his brakes and jerked his steering wheel hard to the right. Completing a 180 degree turn, Mike then took off down the street going forward instead of backward.

With his tires squealing as he negotiated a left turn down Bleeker Street, Mike began to reflect upon the day's events. He now knew that Bruno wasn't infallible. He sometimes seemed to act spontaneously and without deliberate thought to guide his actions. He also seemed to be rather hot-headed and temperamental. Perhaps these were weaknesses Mike could exploit in the future. Mike also wondered about the chocolate connection. There might be some relationship between Bruno's consumption of chocolate and his behavior. Chocolate could be another weakness altogether or a related weakness that Mike might be able to take advantage of sometime.

In thinking over all of this, Mike knew that he eventually would have to decide if pursuing Bruno was the best course of action. Perhaps he should call off his chase and let the police take over (the unmanly thing to do). Or, perhaps, he should use another approach to stalk Bruno (as long as certain manly criteria are satisfied). However, right now he couldn't think of anything in his past that was similar to his present situation. Not when his life was threatened and he also was being stalked by a chocolate-crazed demon like Bruno. As he pulled into the parking place in front of his brownstone apartment building, Mike realized that he did know one thing for certain: A good night's sleep is what he needed now. A sleep to chase away his problems. So far, he had eluded Bruno. But tomorrow was another day.

In learning about Bruno, Mike has begun to construct some general impressions of Bruno's strengths and weaknesses. Each time Mike encounters Bruno, he reacts to certain cues and nuances and files them away for future reference. Eventually, Mike could accumulate enough information to predict Bruno's actions with a reasonably high degree of accuracy. At such a time, Mike's problem with Bruno would be resolved.

There also are certain constraints in Mike's problem situation. The most important of these are the time available to learn about Bruno and the need to take defensive action to prevent Bruno from carrying out his threat to get Mike.

Both of these constraints represent elements of separate problems which probably will require Mike's attention. For example, Mike may evaluate his progress in dealing with his primary problem in terms of the amount of problem-solving time consumed and the amount of time remaining. Thus, he may be unfamiliar with how much time he has available now and how much time he would like to have (a Type VI, Resource/Goal problem). But he also may have ideas for creating more time. Should he develop a satisfactory way of dealing with this subproblem, then one constraint on his major problem will be alleviated. The need to take defensive action is another constraint that could be dealt with in a similar way.

At this point in his stalking process, Mike seems to be dealing with a Transformational/Goal problem (Type IV). He still does not seem to be clear about his primary goal and the transformations needed to develop a problution. His general goal of getting Bruno before he gets him seems clear enough. However, Mike will need to refine this goal to make significant progress toward development of a problution.

The ease with which Mike is able to refine his goal will be determined, in part, by his overall ability to sense his general problem situation and apply a problem-finding strategy. His understanding and familiarity with his problem will be increased if he heightens his awareness by becoming more problem-centered rather than solution-centered (Maier, 1963).

In the previous chapters I have discussed some of the basic elements of problem finding, alternative stalking approaches used in various problem-solving models, and a typology of problems based upon a problem solver's degree of familiarity with three major problem components. In this chapter, I will discuss some basics of the hunt. In particular, I will look at the sensing process required to develop a general understanding of a problem situation. In Chapters Five and Six I will describe the searching elements of the problem-finding process. Then, in the two remaining chapters, I will describe processes for finding problutions (Chapter Seven) and for developing any final transformations needed to close the gap between initial and goal states (Chapter Eight).

This approach is generally consistent with the suggestion of Lyles and Mitroff (1980) that problem formulation involves three primary steps: (1) sensing the existence of a problem, (2) identifying the contributing factors, and (3) reaching a problem definition. After becoming aware that a problem exists, you should attempt to learn about the factors which contributed to your awareness. Once you have done this, it should be relatively easy to develop a problem definition.

Sensing

Before you can understand a problem adequately, you first must be aware of its existence. Then, you must become as familiar as possible with the problem. If you discover that you have a high level of familiarity with your problem, you may decide to terminate the process and develop a solution. Or, you may decide you are not familiar enough with the problem and proceed with additional problem finding. The process underlying these decisions is sensing—attempting to experience as much as possible about the problem. For purposes of convenience, I have divided the sensing process into activities and techniques.

Activities. The sensing process involves several activities. The specific number of them will depend upon how complex you want to make the process. A representative sample of some things you might do are: (1) assess your overall motivation to deal with the general problem situation, (2) evaluate your personal reactions to the

Take a good sniff!!

problem gap you perceive, (3) assess the meanings you give to various problem components and their relation to one another, (4) search your long-term memory to locate any similar problems which might help you evaluate your feelings toward your current problem, and (5) determine if this is a problem you wish to avoid or one you want to meet head on.

Assess your motivation. One of the most important factors in your ability to sense a problem situation is your motivation level. You must have a felt need to solve an ill-structured problem to realistically expect that you can achieve a workable solution. However, this motivation must be internal rather than external. You must want to solve the problem because you want to and not because you are being rewarded or punished by some external source (Amabile, 1983). Thus, you will be more successful at developing problutions if you want to do it and not because your boss, teacher, or friends want you to.

Evaluate your reactions to the problem gap. At the time you perceive a difference between an existing state and a goal state, you might react in a variety of ways. For example, you might feel overwhelmed by the enormity or significance of the problem, feel "underwhelmed" by the lack of importance of the problem, panic when you feel that you cannot possibly begin to resolve the problem in the time available, develop a firm resolve to develop a problution when you understand the problem gap clearly, or begin to think of possible solutions.

Whether you experience one or more of these reactions during the course of dealing with your problem is not all that important. What is important is how you respond to your reactions. In some cases, your responses might affect your motivation to proceed with further problem solving; in other cases, your responses may be neutral and signify nothing relevant about your ability to deal with your problem. In any event, it is important that you try to become aware of reactions you have to different problem situations and how these reactions can affect your ability to deal with your problems.

Some recent research even suggests that how you approach your problems can affect how successful you will be at problem solving. Based upon correlations between subscales of the Problem Solving Inventory (Heppner & Petersen, 1982) and the Coping Strategies Inventory (Heppner, Hibel, Neal, Weinstein & Rabinowitz, 1982), some researchers found that individuals who approach their problems with confidence are more likely to focus on the situation and reframe their problems to make it easier to solve them (Ritchey, Carscaddon & Morgan, 1984). Perhaps the lesson, then, is to try and react positively to your problem situations.

Assess meanings you give to problem components. The activities for assessing meanings you give to problem components are similar to those for evaluating your reactions to the problem gap. The specific process is similar to what has been described already when discussing pattern recognition. Whenever you perceive shapes, forms, textures or smells, you probably ascribe some meaning to them. It is only natural to attempt to make sense out of ambiguous stimulus material. The more you understand your environment, the easier it will be for you to deal with it. The same holds true for problem finding: The more you understand a problem situation, the more likely it is that you will be successful at developing a problution.

When dealing with a problem, the initial state, the goal state, and the potential transformations involved all will have meanings that are probably unique to you. For instance, a particular goal state may evoke memories of previous goals associated with previous problems. Some of these goals (or portions of them) may influence how you perceive a current goal. It is difficult to be totally objective, so you should try to become aware of why you see things as you do. If you become successful at doing this, it will be easier to recognize when your problem perspective is too narrow.

Doing all of this may be easier said than done. Just advising people to evaluate the meanings they give to situations does not mean that they can do it. People sometimes introduce factors into situations which are not really there. That is, if we do not like the reality facing us, we may decide to construct one we do like.

Some research suggests that we also may do something like this during problem solving. For example, Greeno (1976) found that people who are given a well-structured problem tend to introduce problem components different from those initially presented to them. Specifically, they changed the goal state from one that was definite to one that was indefinite; from one that could be satisfied by a specific criterion to one that could be satisfied by a number of different alternatives. It is, of course, unclear about whether or not similar behavior would take place if the initial problem is ill-structured with an indefinite goal. Nevertheless, we should be aware

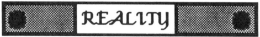

that we may inappropriately change some situations (consciously or unconsciously) to best suit our needs.

Although assessing the meanings you give to problem components may be an important part of the sensing process, it may be more important to assess the relations you perceive to exist among the components. How do you see the current problem state affecting the goal state? The goal state affecting the current state? Potential transformations affecting the current and goal states? In making these and other assessments you need to be aware that your perceptions of any situation probably are interrelated to varying degrees. Although you will have to deal with each component separately, you also will need to keep the total problem situation in mind. This will be discussed in more detail in the next section.

Search your long-term memory. Any patterns you recognize as familiar while evaluating your reactions or assessing meanings to problem components will be determined by what is stored in your long-term memory (Simon, 1973). You cannot recognize something unless you have some degree of familiarity with it. And, any familiarity you might have will be determined by what you can remember. This probably is relatively obvious to you. What may not be quite so obvious is the triggering role long-term memory lays in problem finding.

Your memory is responsible for how you recognize each problem pattern. Moreover, each pattern is a stimulus that helps evoke other patterns. Thus, you originally might perceive a problem situation as a gap between initial state A and goal state B. Recognition of this pattern then might prompt in your memory another pattern such as initial state A and goal state C or initial state D and goal state D. The more you search your long-term memory, the better you will do at sensing the general problem situation. However, not allowing enough time for this search may result in inaccurate or inappropriate perceptions.

Evaluate your approach-avoidance feelings. Depending upon your long-term memory search and your overall feelings about the problem at this point, you may decide that the problem is one you either want to deal with or avoid. Thus, you might feel you absolutely have to solve the problem. Or, you might feel that you should not attempt a solution because of the potential risks involved, a lack of time, or other factors.

According to many researchers (e.g., Bloom & Broder, 1950; Shaftel & Shaftel, 1967), the most successful problem solvers are those who tend to approach rather than avoid their problems. Thus, if you feel a strong need to avoid a problem, you might want to reconsider dealing with it for the time being. Your feelings toward the problem might change if they are allowed to incubate for a while. Then, when you feel less aversive toward the problem, you might try to deal with it again. Of course, you will not always have the luxury of deferring work on all problems. Some problems require immediate attention, so you just will have to take your chances.

Whatever you decide, a final sensing activity is to analyze your feelings about either proceeding or terminating the problem-solving process. This does not have to be a complicated, time-consuming analysis. Rather, it may be more effective if you think about your initial reactions to either proceeding or terminating. Then, quickly try to think of the primary reason you developed these reactions. If you understand why you feel the way you do, it may help you understand why you are looking at your problem from a particular perspective. Then, if you decide that you are using the wrong perspective, you might try another one.

Techniques

In addition to these specific sensing activities, there also are more general techniques you can use to increase your awareness of problem situations. Two broad but basic methods I will discuss here are relaxation and intuition. These very general sensing methods will help attune you to the basic nature of your problems and enable you to view them with the proper perspective.

Relaxation. When things get too stressful and we appear to have trouble dealing with them, people usually tell us to take it easy and relax. The idea is that we can cope better with difficult situations if we are not in a state of frenzy. The same holds true when dealing with ill-structured problems. We can deal with them much more effectively if we are not experiencing undue stress. That is, if we are in control of our thinking abilities, we can more effectively handle ambiguous situations we experience as stressful. This probably holds true even if these situations are only minimally stressful, as is the case with many ill-structured problems.

There is some research available which supports the notion that stress affects our ability to think and process information. For example, Holsti (1971) found that people tend to screen out essential information during decision making when they are under stress. Levine (1971) observed that people make poorer quality deci-

sions when cognitive efficiency is decreased. And re-searchers such as Beier (1951) have found that stress promotes a rigidity in problem solving that makes it difficult for people to do abstract reasoning and tolerate ambiguity.

To counter the negative aspects of stress, relaxation techniques are frequently proposed as remedies (e.g., Davis, McKay & Eshelman, 1980). One simple procedure uses breathing to help induce a more relaxed state. Begin by sitting in a comfortable chair or by lying on the floor. Close your eyes, take a deep breath, and exhale slowly while thinking about all the tension leaving your body. Next, slowly repeat this breathing procedure for different parts of your body (e.g. shoulders, chest, stomach, thighs, calves, feet). Each time you exhale, think about how you are becoming more and more relaxed. Then, once you have achieved a desired level of relaxation, try to deal with your problem.

Intuition. The intuitive process is frequently associated with the creative process. Very creative people often are viewed as being very intuitive. Although this may be true, intuition probably does not "cause" creativity or vice versa. Your intuitive abilities may help you solve problems creatively and your creative abilities may help you solve problems intuitively. However, this does not mean that one is the direct cause of the other.

Unquestionably, creativity is facilitated by intuition, but it is more than likely determined by a whole constellation of traits, skills, abilities, attitudes, needs, etc. in addition to intuition. Thus, it might be more appropriate to say that intuition is "associated" with creativity and creative problem solving. However, intuition is not creativity or an end product of creativity. Intuition is a means to achieve creative products.

Using our intuition to understand intuition can lead to misguided conclusions (in much the same way as using our brains to study our brains may be limiting). As a result, what cannot be easily explained often is passed off as being due to intuition. For example, you may have made an important decision in your life which you later judged to be very creative. As you reflect more on this decision, you may discover that you really don't know why it turned out as well as it did. At the time, you may have concentrated on only a few areas and quickly made some evaluations without really knowing why you made them. The outcome may have seemed to be both mysterious and miraculous. However, it also may be that your actions were guided unconsciously by well thought out behaviors.

The difference between creativity and intuition probably is not as important as the realization that intuition is involved in the creative problem-solving process. And, its role in this process is probably no more important than during problem finding. Whenever you think, you are using your intuition to some degree, whether you are aware of it or not. You "find" too many problems every day to rely exclusively upon a rational model of problem finding. If you are human, you are not a totally rational being who solves problems using only analytical thinking processes. Of necessity, there are times when you must allow intuition to guide you when dealing with novel or unfamiliar situations.

An excellent definition of intuition is Isenberg's (1984). According to Isenberg, intuition is "the smooth automatic peformance of learned behavior sequences" (p.85). This means that intuitive thinking skills may appear at times to be mystical (as we often view creativity), but they actually originate with previous behaviors that may be very analytical and even rational.

When you act intuitively, you are behaving in a "natural" way, based upon your previous conditioning in a similar situation. In this regard, intuitive thinking is almost a reflexive action. Confronted with certain cues in your environment, you respond almost without thinking. You are "programmed" by past experience to respond in a certain way. As Isenberg notes, "years of experience and learning are compressed into split seconds" (p.83).

During problem finding, you should use your intuition to help you recognize and clarify problem components. Your intuitive abilities provide you with an ideal mechanism for collecting and synthesizing apparently unrelated bits of data and transforming them into an integrated whole. While playing around with bits of data, patterns should begin to emerge which were not previously apparent. And, relationships should form about how the problem components are related. As this process unfolds, your understanding of the problem situation should increase.

This is not to say that you would not be using your intuition anyway. It is almost impossible for you to not think intuitively during problem solving. Depending upon your experience with a problem, you probably use your intuitive skills in varying amounts. The point is that you should not be afraid to rely upon your intuition. It is too valuable a resource to write off simply because it cannot be quantified or measured.

Bruno's hands tightened their grip around Mike's neck. Squeezing tighter and tighter, Mike felt Bruno's hands shutting off his last breath of air. Bells began to chime and lights began to flash. Tilt!

Mike suddenly felt himself falling and then tumbling— tumbling down a torrid river, buffeted against the soft, brown rocks. The next thing he knew, his head was going under and a thick liquid began forcing its way into his mouth and nose. With his breathing becoming more labored, Mike kicked his legs and managed to thrust his head upward to take in a quick breath. Then, submerged once again, he knew what was in his mouth: Chocolate . . . apparently a fine Swiss variety. It started to fill every orifice in Mike's body, choking off all life in him. He knew he was doomed.

Coughing and sputtering, Mike opened his eyes and found himself in his bedroom staring at the designer-spattered brown paint on his walls. So, it only had been a nightmare. Tell that to his sore neck and clogged breathing passages!

Shaking off the nuisance of the night and reaching for a nearby nosespray, Mike began planning for the day ahead. Foremost on his mind was finding Bruno. He now felt more confident about his ability to get Bruno. The problem no longer felt quite so overwhelming, especially since he learned of Bruno's apparent addiction to chocolate. Mike now believed that his goal was beginning to crystallize. Simply catching and holding Bruno for the authorities seemed paramount. It may change tomorrow, but for today the goal seemed realistic.

Closing his eyes, Mike leaned back in his easy chair and began searching his past for possible solutions. He remembered how, as a boy, he and his father would put out salt blocks in the woods nearby their house. Deer from miles around would be attracted and lick the blocks. Perhaps there was something here to spark an idea on how Bruno might "take his licks," too! That's it, thought Mike. Attract Bruno and then catch him. Now, what would attract a chocoholic? Hmmm?

As Mike mused over his question, he thought he heard a scream for help coming from the street below. Rushing to his window, he saw her.

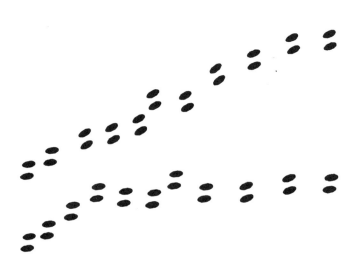

CHAPTER FIVE: PREPARING FOR THE CHASE

REDEFINITIONAL TECHNIQUES

Looking out his bedroom window, Mike immediately recognized the woman in distress. It was Mitzi, Bruno's girl.
The last time Mike saw Mitzi was when he had followed
her to her apartment. However, the only thing he gained
from his sleuthing then was a king size goose egg. That
and a headache which throbbed for two days.

Right now, Mitzi was down on her knees and in
trouble. A large, hulking figure was standing over her,
slapping her and screaming something about how she
was going to get what she deserved. Mike went to his
dresser, opened a drawer, and pulled out the .357 mag-
num he kept with his underwear.

Flinging open his window, he shouted, "Hey, why
doncha pick on someone your own size?" With that snappy
admonishment, Mike fired three shots into the pavement
next to the hulking figure. Thunk! Plink! Thunk! As soon
as the chewed pavement began flying about, the hulk
turned tail and ran, just as all bullies do. Mike shouted
again, this time to Mitzi. "Hold on! I'll be right down."

When Mike reached Mitzi, she fell sobbing into his
arms. After trying to console her, he learned that the
hulk was one of Bruno's friends. Bruno apparently had
sent him to rough up Mitzi a little for something she had
said. She really didn't know what she had said that would
have upset Bruno so much. In any event, Mike suggested
that she come up to his place to calm down.

Once in his apartment, Mike fixed coffee for them
and they sat down on the chairs next to his kitchen table.
After a few minutes of casual conversation, he learned
that Mitzi first met Bruno when they worked together
at the Beano Corporation. After listening to the details
of their courtship, Mike eventually learned that Beano
manufactures gourmet chocolate candies!

It was at that moment that Mike had one of those
sudden insights which can strike when you least expect
them. If both Bruno and Mitzi are chocoholics, Mike might
be able to use that information to set a trap for Bruno.

And Mitzi, with her inside knowledge of the chocolate industry, would be just the person to help him! Moreover, she now had the motivation to help Mike: Revenge for Bruno's most recent dastardly deed. By joining together, both Mike and Mitzi could benefit. Now, all they needed was a plan. A plan devious, yet simple enough for Bruno to fall easily into their hands.

Mike's knowledge and understanding about Bruno's behavior seem to have increased to the point where a specific plan of action could begin to take shape. Ever since starting this case, Mike has been guided by some form of a plan. However, each new encounter with Bruno (or others involved in the situation) required a refinement in planning. As a result, Mike has continually adjusted his perceptions and his overall approach to dealing with Bruno during his search for new information.

Mike's definition of his problem also has been altered somewhat. Mike now is concerned with developing ways to lure Bruno into a trap. The initial and goal states of his problem have become fairly clear to him. All that remains is to develop transformations to close the gap between the problem states (a Type II problem—Pure Transformational).

In this chapter, I will describe two techniques to help in further redefining the general problem situation. Assuming that sensing has increased your overall problem awareness, you now should be ready for the searching phase of the problem-finding process. In this phase you should try to develop specific problem redefinitions and make note of any potential subproblems. Then, you will need to narrow down your list of redefinitions and select the best one for your final transformations of the initial and goal problem states.

The two redefinitional techniques I will describe in this chapter have been used for years as part of the five-step Creative Problem-Solving approach of Parnes,

Noller, and Biondi (1977). I refer to these techniques as the "Five Ws" and "Why?" methods. Both involve fact-finding and problem-finding activities which can help to increase familiarity with your problems.

Five W's Method. Recognizing the patterns you see in problem situations requires recall of previous information. The number and variety of patterns you can recognize will be determined directly by the amount and type of information you have stored in your long-term memory. As you search this memory, pull out information, and organize it into patterns, you progressively reduce the number of patterns available to you. There are only so many different ways you can organize information, given the limitations of the human mind.

For example, consider a problem involving ways to increase your income. You might think of ten general ways people use to get more money (transformations), three ways which you could use to describe your current income level (initial states), and six ways to describe desired income levels (goal states). Thus, you might develop a list containing: (1) transformation ideas (e.g., get a second job, write a book, develop an investment portfolio); (2) initial state information (e.g., current annual income, current income plus benefits, method of payment for current income); and (3) goal state information (e.g., desired annual income, desired sources of annual income, alternative definitions of income).

Different combinations of these ways to bring about transformations and information about initial and goal states would increase the total number of possibilities (patterns) even more. However, once you have examined all the possibilities, you will have exhausted the number of problem patterns you can deal with in developing a problution. In other words, you are limited by the information available to you.

To overcome the limitations of your memory and your ability to process and acquire information, it would help if you had some way to stimulate your memory. In most cases, your available information is not limited by what you know, but by what you can access from what you know. That is, you know a lot more than you can recall upon demand. Increasing your awareness and understanding of your problems then becomes a matter of accessing more information from your memory. This is what the Five W's method is designed to do. (Obviously, I am not suggesting that this technique is the only way to access information from your memory.)

The five W's are: Who? What? Where? When? and Why? questions. How? also can be added to these as a supplemental question. All of these are basic types of questions to help overcome some of the limitations of the human mind. By using each question to draw out the information in your memory, you will be actively sensing many different dimensions of your problem situation. Then, once you have looked over your responses to these questions, a clearer picture of the problem may emerge. The picture may not always be sufficient to suggest a problution, but it should make it easier to know how to proceed in developing one.

To use this technique in a more or less systematic way, you should begin by asking many different questions about your problem. Each of these questions should begin with one of the stimulator words. After you have asked a question (or, actually at any point during the process), you should write down whatever responses you think of. Do this without judging either your questions or your responses. Deferred judgment is especially important during fact-finding and problem-finding, since you do not want to be limited by any artificial constraints you might place upon a situation. Finally, look over all of your responses, and write down any new problem definitions which might pop into your mind. Again, try not to judge any of these definitions and try to think of as many as you can. An example should help illustrate this process.

Suppose you describe your general problem situation as: IWWMW encourage people to stop littering the highways by throwing things out of their cars? Using the five W and how questions, you might set up an analysis of this situation as follows:

Who Questions
1. Who litters the highways?
2. Who picks up the litter?
3. Who does not litter the highways?
4. Who watches other people litter the highways?
5. Who could catch people before they litter the highways?

What Questions
1. What is litter?
2. What if litter rebounded into cars as soon as it was thrown?
3. What is littered the most
4. What is littered the least?
5. What are people who litter afraid of?

PLEASE
DO NOT LITTER

Where Questions
1. Where do people usually litter?
2. Where do people rarely litter?
3. Where is litter least likely to be picked up?
4. Where do people obtain their litter?
5. Where should people dispose of their trash?

When Questions
1. When do people litter most?
2. When do people litter least?
3. When is litter picked up?
4. When is litter most likely to be noticed?
5. When is litter least likely to be noticed?

How Questions
1. How is litter picked up?
2. How is litter disposed of once it is picked up?
3. How do most people start to litter?
4. How would people respond if individuals who littered were shot as soon as they threw something out a car window?
5. How do people decide what to litter?

Using these questions as stimuli, I have generated sample responses you might use to gain a different problem perspective. Of course, there are many more possible responses and you may be able to think of entirely different ones.

Who Question Responses
1. Thoughtless people; people who are unconcerned with the appearance of the highways; people who would rather litter the highways than their cars.
2. State and city highway crews; volunteer groups and organizations; concerned individual citizens; prisoner work gangs.
3. Considerate people; people previously arrested

and fined for littering; people with total physical disabilities.
4. Police; other motorists; an individual's conscience.
5. Other people in the cars of people who litter; people driving near them; people standing next to the highway; people flying over the highway in airplanes or helicopters.

What Question Responses
1. Any object thrown out of a car; trash; unwanted material; junk.
2. When police are nearby; in heavy traffic; when there is nothing inside their cars to litter; when they believe they are likely to get caught.
3. Aluminum cans; paper wrappers; bottles.
4. Television sets in working order; airplanes; new stereo systems; people; Renoir paintings; diamond rings.
5. Getting caught; getting fined; the sky falling.

Where Question Responses
1. In the grass; where traffic is relatively light; on the pavement.
2. Where there are a lot of police; in communities where there is a lot of pride in environmental appearance.
3. In deep ravines; in rivers; any treacherous area; where there is little community pride; where motivation, volunteer spirit, or money is low.
4. Stores; other people; what previously used to be litter; trash piles.
5. Trash cans in stores and rest areas; bags kept in cars.

When Questions Responses
1. When tired; when lazy; when no one else is around; when just finished eating or drinking.

2. When police are nearby; in heavy traffic; when there is nothing inside their cars to litter; when they believe they are likely to get caught.
3. When people are motivated; when prisoners and volunteers do it; when people who litter are caught and forced to do it.
4. When it is shiny; when it is large; when it is in great quantities; when it is dramatically different from its surroundings.
5. When it is small in size; when it is small in quantity; when it is hidden in tall grass; when the view is attractive enough to draw attention away from the litter.

Why Question Responses
1. To avoid trashing their cars; because they don't expect to get caught; because they have no clear-cut motivation not to litter.
2. Parental upbringing; a concern for and appreciation of the environment; fear of being caught; because they carry trash bags in their cars; because they prefer to litter inside of their cars.
3. To keep the environment nice looking and safe; to reduce costs to city and state governments and ultimately to the taxpayers; because it can endanger human lives when thrown or blown onto other cars.
4. It is too difficult to reach; it cannot be seen; the officials responsible do not have enough money; people lack the motivation.
5. The people responsible take pride in their environment; violators of littering laws are punished immediately by having to pick up litter; people who are seen littering are shot.

How Question Responses
1. By hand; by machine; by metal-pointed sticks; by

concerned people; by coerced people.
2. By burning; burying; recycling; by transportation in trucks to another location so it becomes someone else's problem.
3. By watching their parents do it; by watching respected peers do it; by noticing how much litter already exists; to retaliate against authority.
4. With shock; with amazement; with unbelieving eyes; by reporting such incidents to the police; by joining in.
5. By what they happen to have in their cars at the time; by what their passengers bring with them; by the size of the object; by the value of the object to them.

In looking over all of these responses, you should be able to develop a variety of problem redefinitions. Some of these may be very general and somewhat vague, while others may be in the form of problutions. For example, using the responses above, I was able to develop the following 24 redefinitions:

In what ways might:
1. people become more concerned about the appearance of the highways?
2. people be made more aware of the consequences of littering?
3. police catch more people in the act of littering?
4. occupants of cars encourage each other not to litter?
5. airplanes and helicopters be used to catch people littering?
6. people be encouraged to put litter bags in their cars and use them?
7. people be encouraged to litter only material that can be picked up easily?
8. people be rewarded for not littering and reporting people who do litter?

9. certain portions of a highway be designated as areas for littering?
10. more police or other authorities be used to patrol for littering?
11. community pride be used to prevent littering?
12. money be raised for litter prevention programs?
13. product manufacturers encourage people not to litter?
14. litter be blended in with its environment?
15. people who litter be made to feel as if someone is watching for littering at all times?
16. car manufacturers be encouraged to install built-in litter disposal units in vehicles?
17. car windows be designed to encourage people to discard objects of only a specified size?
18. scenery appear to be so attractive that only the lowest "scum" would even consider littering?
19. parents be motivated to encourage their children not to litter?
20. people be protected in their cars from potential damage caused by litter thrown out of another car's windows?
21. litter be made more accessible for picking up?
22. radar be used to detect littering of metallic material?
23. cars be inspected at special "litter stations" along a highway?
24. small mountains of litter be placed at certain intervals along a highway to make people more aware of the problem?

The information provided by these redefinitions should be extremely useful to help you sense and further understand the general problem situation. What is particularly useful about these definitions, however, is that you may perceive some of them to be potential solutions rather than simple problem restatements. You also might see some of them as approximate solutions. Or, you even may find that some of the redefinitions are more on the opposite end of the scale for you, existing as broader redefinitions of the original problem statement.

Your redefinitions may exist on a scale ranging from low solution specificity at one end to high specificity at the other end. **Figure 5-1** illustrates this situation. In this case, you may see some of the redefinitions as poorly defined solutions, such as the rabbit at the left. At other times, you may see the rabbit specified more fully, such as the one at the far right (represented here as a problution), or somewhere in between. Whatever your perceptions, the patterns you see are solutions which vary only in the amount of information (familiarity) you have about them.

Your redefinitions also might lie on a scale where the endpoints represent different degrees of problem specificity. That is, you might perceive the problems you

Figure 5-1. Solution specificity continuum.

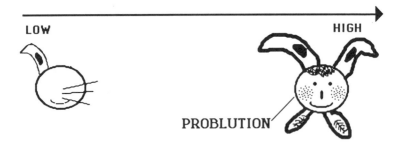

encounter as clearly specified (a well-structured problem or problution) or not clearly specified. These latter problems all can be classified as ill-structured, as long as a solution is not evident to you whenever you are dealing with the problem situation. Such a situation could be illustrated using a figure identical to **Figure 5-1**, except that the variable represented would be perceived problems instead of perceived solutions. Thus, problem specificity could range from low to high.

Because of the interrelated nature of problems and solutions, it is also possible to think of solutions and problems as existing on two separate, yet interacting and dynamic continua. For instance, you initially may perceive a poorly structured problem, then a poorly specified solution, and finally a well-structured solution. Along the way, there could be many deadends and revised perceptions. A graphic representation of such a situation is shown in **Figure 5-2**.

Figure 5-2 Problem and solution continua based upon specificity.

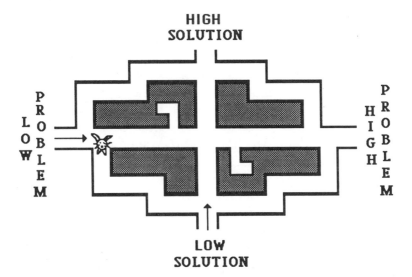

Just as an example, if you start with a problem low in specificity (a "low" problem) and move to a "low" solution (i.e., your perceptions change to a "low" solution), you might end up developing a "high" solution or problution. It also is possible that you might proceed from a low problem, to a low solution, and then to a high problem which, of course, also would be a problution. No matter how you proceed, your objective is to reach either a high solution or problem.

To illustrate how this procedure might operate at a very general level, suppose you begin with little information about the problem states or the needed transformations. If you are unfamiliar with the problem, it would be a "low" problem. As you acquire more information and increase your problem familiarity, a solution may begin to take shape in your mind. If this solution is not well specified and one with which you are not familiar, it could be classified as a low solution. Increasing the amount of information you gather then might change your perceptions to a well-defined situation with high familiarity. In this case, you would have transformed an ill-defined solution (a "low" solution) into a well-defined problem definition. Such a situation would be a high problem as well as a problution, since the problem components would be familiar and you only would need to complete the required transformations to resolve the situation.

Regardless of where your redefinitions lie on different scales at the outset, you can use redefinitions to help you better understand the broader problem situation. The solutions which appear to you now might even be applied successfully later on if you decide upon a pure transformational problem (i.e., a Type II problem characterized by familiar initial and goal states and unfamiliar transformations), which normally precedes development of a problution. As shown in **Figure 5-2**, you could begin with a low solution and proceed directly to a high solution. If you consider this solution to be tentative and you have time to work on the problem, you then might gather enough information to develop a high problem. In other words, you could change from one form of problution to another.

To illustrate how you might organize your redefinitions to help increase your problem understanding, I have categorized the 24 redefinitions I generated according to the problem types presented in **Table 3-1**.

As I view them, redefinitions 5, 6, 9, 10, 22, 23, and 24 are Type I problems (Well-structured problems or problutions); redefinitions 1, 8, 12, 13, 16, 19, 21, and 7 seem to be Type II problems (Pure Transformational problems, where the initial and goal states are familiar); redefinitions 2, 11, 14, 15, 17, 18, and 20 appear to be Type IV problems (Transformational/Goal problems in which only the initial state is familiar); and redefinition 4 is a Type VI problem (a Resource/Transformational problem, in which the goal state is familiar).

I must emphasize that these classifications represent how I would categorize the problem redefinitions. You may have an entirely different perspective, depending upon your general knowledge, motivation and attitude toward the original problem. As with the basic problem-finding process, the accuracy of your problem classifications are not as important as how you use the classifications to help develop problutions.

This particular grouping of redefinitions suggests some general directions about how you might proceed in further dealing with the littering problem. The most obvious direction would be to treat all of the Type I redefinitions as problutions waiting to be implemented. For example, redefinition 5 (using helicopters and airplanes to catch people littering) and redefinition 6 (encouraging people to put litter bags in their cars) both could be viewed as existing solutions. All that is needed is to decide which problems would work best and then devise an implementation plan.

The redefinitions grouped as Type II problems would require more work than those classified as Type I problems. Type II or transformational problems require that operators be devised for reducing the gap perceived to exist between the initial and goal problem states. For example, redefinition number 12 implies that not enough money is available for litter prevention programs. Once ways are developed to produce the necessary money, this problem could be resolved.

The redefinitions classified as Type IV problems represent an entirely different situation from the first two problem types. These problems assume that the initial problem state is relatively well-specified and familiar to the problem solver, but the goal state and the necessary transformation are more ill-defined. Generally speaking, before any transformations can be developed, the goal first must be clarified. Then, major attention can be given to devising the needed transformations.

A Type IV problem situation can be illustrated by looking at redefinition number 11. This particular redefinition deals with designing ways of using community pride to prevent littering. By leaving open the required level and quality of community pride (the goal state), transformation cannot be developed until the goal state is decided upon. Assuming that the current level of community pride is relatively well-known, the initial state should be familiar to the problem solver. Therefore, only the type and quality of pride needed to prevent littering would be problematic. Once this goal is clarified, the remaining task is to generate ways to make the current level of pride more like the goal state. However, it would not be unusual to find that clarifying the goal state allows a problution to emerge and be selected as the best solution.

The final category of redefinitions from this illustration contains only redefinition number 4, which was classified as a Type VI problem (a Resource/Transformation problem). In this instance, the goal state is well-specified or familiar, but the initial state is not familiar and the transformations are unspecified (or it is not apparent what they might be).

This redefinition involves developing ways for passengers to encourage each other to stop littering. In this case, I assumed that I was unclear about how people currently encourage each other to stop littering. Although I have a fair idea of what might be involved in the current state, I was much less certain about how they *should* encourage each other to stop littering. That is, I had some uncertainty about how people actually encourage each other now (the initial state), but I had significantly greater uncertainty about the type of encouragement needed to effectively prevent littering (the goal state). The actual behaviors involved, of course, would be open to debate. In fact, I just as easily could have classified this redefinition as a Type II problem. I did not do so, since I had a minimal level of uncertainty about the initial state.

At this point in the process, you will need to make a decision about the next step to take. One alternative would be to select one or more of the definitions categorized as Type I problems and follow it through to implementation. A second alternative would be to continue problem finding using an existing or modified problem from those not classified as problutions. A third alternative would be to try to develop additional redefinitions. This could be done through a little individual brainstorming or by using another technique.

Why Method. If you are not completely satisfied with any of your redefinitions generated from the Five W's Method, you can try the Why Method. This technique is especially useful if you are experiencing any uncertainty about your familiarity and understanding of the problem situation. In particular, if you are not confident that you have tested your major assumptions about the larger problem situation, you probably would want to use this technique.

The major objective of the Why Method is to broaden your overall problem perspective. To understand any problem fully, you must push it to its limits so you know its boundaries. A simple exercise I sometimes use in creative problem-solving workshops should help illustrate this point.

Have someone select a picture about the size of a standard sheet of paper. Don't let them show it to you. Close your eyes and have them hold the paper in front of your face so it touches your nose. Open your eyes and describe what you see. You shouldn't be able to recognize the picture at this distance. Then, close your eyes again. Have your helper hold the paper just far enough away so you can't tell what the picture is. Open your eyes and again try to describe what you see. Assuming that you can't recognize the picture because of its distance from you, ask your partner to slowly move the picture toward you, about three feet at a time. Have your partner stop when you finally are able to recognize the picture.

The perspective you need to recognize the picture exists somewhere between your nose and the farthest distance the picture was from you. If recognizing the picture was the problem in this exercise, then the far and near distances the picture was held from you represent the problem's boundaries. For you to solve this problem, the picture had to be placed somewhere within the boundaries that are meaningful to you.

Just as your eyesight and ability to recognize certain types of pictures may differ from other people, the way you initially represent your problems may differ from other people. Sometimes you may recognize a particular problem considerably faster than someone else. And, the reverse also may be true. We all operate with different sets of perceptual filters. When we are blinded by these filters, relatively structured techniques often can help. The Why Method is one such technique which can help you broaden a problem by testing its boundaries.

The basic steps involved in using the Why Method are: (1) state your original problem definition, (2) ask "Why?" you want to do whatever is contained in the definition, (3) restate the problem using your response, and (4) repeat this procedure with each new redefinition until you achieve a level of abstraction which makes it impractical to continue. A couple of examples using the littering problem can help illustrate this technique.

Problem:	IWWMW encourage people to stop littering the highways by throwing things out of their cars?
Ask Why?	Why do we want to encourage people to stop littering the highways by throwing things out of their cars?
Answer:	To make it easier to enjoy the scenery.
Restate:	IWWMW make it easier for people to enjoy the scenery?
Ask Why?:	Why do we want people to enjoy the scenery?
Answer:	So they can appreciate the esthetic aspects of our environment.
Restate:	IWWMW help people appreciate the esthetic aspects of our environment?

At this point, you may decide that: (1) you have redefined the problem as broadly as possible, (2) you are dissatisfied with all the redefinitions you have generated so far and want to explore some others, or (3) you are dissatisfied with the redefinitions so far and want to try a different approach. If you believe you have broadened the problem as much as needed, you could terminate the process and select one of the redefinitions for further use. If one or more redefinitions appear to you in the form of problutions, you could proceed with solution selection and implementation. If you decide you need to continue with the technique, do so until you reach a definition which seems to be as abstract as possible. However, if you believe that none of the redefinitions are right for the problem situation—if you seem to being going in the wrong direction with the technique, you might want to start again, using a different answer to your first question.

For example, you might have dealt with the same problem situation as follows:

Problem:	IWWMW encourage people to stop littering the highways by throwing things out of their cars?
Ask Why?:	Why do we want to encourage people to stop littering the highways by throwing things out of their cars?
Answer:	To save the money it costs to pick up litter.
Restate:	IWWMW save money picking up litter?
Ask Why?:	Why do we want to save money picking up litter?
Answer:	To have more money available for sewers and education.

You could continue this way or start again using a different answer for the first question. If none of these questions seem to be working for you, you might try a slightly different approach to the Why Method. Instead of asking why you want to do something, try asking why something is done. Thus, instead of asking why you want to encourage people to stop littering, you might ask: Why do people litter? From this point you might deal with the situation as follows:

Answer:	Some people are basically lazy when it comes to litter.
Restate:	IWWMW help people overcome their laziness about litter?
Ask Why?:	Why do you want to help people overcome their laziness about litter?
Answer:	To stop them from littering the highways by throwing things out of their cars.

We now have come full circle with the technique. In this case, you might select the redefinition dealing with helping people overcome their laziness. Or, there may be other definitions you can think of which you would like to consider. However, if you still are dissatisfied with your understanding of the problem and feel that you are not getting close to a problution, there are other techniques you can try. These supplemental redefinitional techniques will be described in the next chapter.

Mike and Mitzi spent most of the night awash in the flowing juices of their creativity. As they plotted and planned their push to punish Bruno, they realized that it wouldn't be easy taking on an opponent as formidable as Bruno. Many people had tried and ended up dead, or worse. Those that came close to giving Bruno his due were those who managed to keep the proper perspective in mind. They knew the type of problem they faced and how to deal with it.

The one question Mike and Mitzi kept asking over and over again was: Why? Why was Bruno doing this to them? Why couldn't anyone stop Bruno? Why did Bruno react so strangely to chocolate? Why did Mike continue to pursue Bruno at great risk to himself? Why are we asking so many questions?

Mitzi looked deep into Mike's eyes, paused briefly to ponder her words and then said, "We need answers, not so many stupid questions."

Mike turned toward Mitzi, tipped his hat back, wet his upper lip with his tongue, and replied, "Answers can't exist without questions."

Casting her eyes downward, Mitzi nodded her head in agreement. She knew he was right. She only needed to hear him say what he said.

Mike moved toward Mitzi and wrapped his left arm around her shoulders. While guiding her toward his front door, he impulsively stopped and grabbed both of her shoulders. And then they kissed, but only briefly. Mike had too many things on his mind now to get involved with a dame.

After Mitzi left, Mike sauntered over to his refrigerator and opened the door to grab a quick beer. As soon as the inside light went on and Mike began reaching for a cold one, he saw something other than his beer. Instead of six packs scattered upon the top shelf, Mike was greeted by a face. A very familiar face.

CHAPTER SIX : MORE CHASE PREPARATIONS

SUPPLEMENTAL
REDEFINITIONAL
TECHNIQUES

The face that greeted Mike in his refrigerator was familiar. It was the same face he saw everyday when shaving. It was his face . . . stuck on a finely-sculpted, full-scale, brown-colored bust. Looking closer, Mike noticed that the bust was not made of clay. No, this bust was carefully crafted from rich, Belgian milk chocolate.

Mike grabbed a can of beer, closed the refrigerator door on his face, and collapsed into his easy chair. He began to reflect upon the events of the past few hours. Who would go to all the trouble to make a bust in his likeness, sneak it into his apartment, and then into his refrigerator? More importantly, why would anyone do this? What did they hope to accomplish? He doesn't particularly care for chocolate. The bust, however, was a flattering likeness. He would have to acknowledge that much.

The only possible answer was that it was meant to be a warning. The question was, what kind of warning? A warning that he was getting too close to Bruno? A warning to keep away from Mitzi? A warning that it just as easily could have been his own flesh and bone head in his refrigerator?

Gulping down the rest of his beer, Mike tossed the can into a nearby trash can, tilted back his head, and sighed. He and Mitzi had agreed to meet that night at Angelo's Ristoranti to begin mapping out an offensive strategy to get Bruno. However, before they could do this, they needed to gather a lot more information about Bruno.

Mike's musings suddenly were interrupted rather abruptly. Bright lights appeared before his eyes. Flashing, multi-colored lights. And, along with the lights was the pain. The pain that was now spreading throughout his skull and shooting down his spine. He suddenly felt sleepy. Nothing but darkness remained.

For most problems, the "Five W's" and "Why" methods will be more than adequate for increasing problem understanding. Depending upon the degree of problem familiarity achieved, a problution may result or you may be several steps closer to developing one. There will be situations, however, in which you may have trouble drawing any closer to a problution. When this occurs, there are several additional methods for stimulating problem familiarity. Not all of these will work for every problem. Nevertheless, one insight or "aha!" is all that is needed to develop a problution.

The need to look at additional redefinitional techniques is underscored by some recent research on problem solving and formulation. Smilansky (1984) obtained results suggesting that the formulation of problems is more difficult than problem solving with a given problem (i.e., a problem that is presented to you to solve). He concluded that problem solving is a necessary but not sufficient ability for problem inventing. To formulate problems, you need the ability to solve given problems. To be an effective problem solver, however, you don't have to be effective at formulating problems.

If it can be assumed that most of us are better at solving given problems than at discovering or inventing problems, then we should welcome any techniques which help us formulate problems better. The techniques in this chapter are designed to do that. Although most of these techniques originally were developed to assist in generating ideas, they can be equally useful in generating problem definitions.

Two Words. Words provide meaning and diversity to our thoughts and the way we communicate. By simply changing key words in a problem statement, a new perspective might be gained. A slight variation in wording may be all that is necessary to help you recall information needed to clarify a problem.

To develop alternate problem definitions with this technique (Olson, 1980), begin by selecting two key words in your initial problem statement. For example, in the litter problem, you might select the words "stop" and "littering." Next, list alternate meanings to each of these words (a thesaurus can help with these lists). In doing this, correctness is not important. Thus, for the word stop you might list: terminate, end, desist, refrain, avoid, hold back, quit. Then, for the word littering, you might list: messing, trashing, unlawfully disposing, spoiling the environment, cluttering. Then, take a word from the first list and combine it with a word from the second list. Examine this combination to see if a useful redefinition either presents itself or is suggested. Continue doing this until you have examined all possible combinations of words from the two lists.

Using the words in this example, you might develop such redefinitions as IWWMW encourage people to: Terminate messing? Refrain from cluttering? Terminate unlawful disposing? End messing?

If none of these redefinitions is satisfactory, you could try using them as stimuli for generating other redefinitions. For instance, the first set of redefinitions might suggest such new redefinitions as IWWMW encourage people to: Clean up their litter? Use trash bags in their cars? Help preserve the environment? Dispose of their trash at certain intervals along the highway?

After examining all of the redefinitions suggested by using the words "stop" and "littering," you also might consider using two other words or phrases in the problem statement. For this problem, you might examine possible combinations using the words "encourage" and "people." The process for using these words would be the same as that used in the previous example.

Reversals. Most police departments continuously deal with the problem of how to catch criminals. In the last few years, some law enforcement agencies have been able to solve some difficult cases by simply reversing this basic law enforcement problem. That is, instead of developing ways to go out and catch criminals, they change the focus to developing ways to get criminals to come to them. The resulting change in perspective led to such innovative solutions as "sting" operations and special "parties" in which limousines were dispatched to criminals who responded to invitations the police sent. The limousines then took the invitees directly to jail (without collecting $200).

Reversing a problem statement involves altering its

perspective in any way possible. There is no "correct" way to reverse a problem statement (de Bono, 1971). To illustrate, a problem of developing ways to increase parking space for shoppers might be redefined as IWWMW: Decrease space for shoppers? Eliminate space for shoppers? Increase space for sellers? Decrease space for sellers? and so forth. These redefinitions then would be used to suggest solutions to the problem.

For instance, decreasing space for shoppers might suggest increasing the number of spaces by decreasing the size of individual parking spaces. Thus, a problem initially perceived as increasing something, might be solved by viewing it, instead, as a problem involving how to decrease something.

Assumption Reversals. Another way to broaden perspectives is to use a technique similar to the Reversals method. According to Grossman (1984), this technique is used by first listing several basic assumptions about the general problem situation. These assumptions should be so obvious that you do not need to consider them at a conscious level. Then, reverse the direction of each assumption, just as was done with the Reversals technique. Finally, use each reversal for possible stimulation of ideas.

To illustrate this technique, consider a problem central to this book: IWWMW encourage people to spend more time defining their problems? Some basic assumptions about this problem might be:

- People assume they know what their problems are.
- People tend to generate ideas without taking time to analyze their problems.
- Some problems require more defining than others.
- It takes more time to define a problem and generate ideas than to just generate ideas.

Reversing some of these assumptions results in

such statements as:
- People never assume they know what their problems are.
- People take time to analyze their problems carefully.
- People understand all of their problems equally well.
- It takes the same amount of time to define problems and generate ideas as it does just to generate ideas.

Using these statements as stimuli, you then might generate a list of redefinitions. Some possible redefinitions include: IWWM people be encouraged to test assumptions they make about their problems? IWWM people feel compelled to analyze their problems before generating ideas? IWWM people use elements common to all problems to produce better solutions? IWWM people make higher quality problem solutions?

Relational Algorithms. The techniques described previously help produce new problem perspectives by changing meanings through word substitutions. The method, known as Relational Algorithms (Crovitz, 1970) can also be used to provoke redefinitions. However, instead of altering words in the original definition, the Relational Algorithms method adds words to the definition. Crovitz suggests using 42 relational words:

about	at	for	of	round	to
across	because	from	off	still	under
after	before	if	on	so	up
against	between	in	opposite	then	when
among	but	near	or	though	where
and	by	not	out	through	while
as	down	now	over	till	with

To this list, I have added 19 prepositions which can also

be used as relational words (VanGundy, 1981):

above	below	except	toward
along	beneath	into	upon
amid	beside	past	within
around	beyond	since	without
behind	during	throughout	

New redefinitions then are generated by selecting two major elements of the original definition, inserting one of the relational words between these elements, and examining this combination for possible stimulation of new redefinitions. Another relational word is selected, the combination examined for any redefinitions stimulated, and so forth, until all the relational words have been inserted and all combinations examined.

To illustrate, consider the problem of increasing parking space for shoppers. The words "parking" and "space" could be selected as the two major elements. Inserting each of the relational words then would result in such combinations as: parking-about-a space, parking-across-a space, parking-after-a space, et cetera. After reviewing all possible combinations, redefinitions might be generated such as:

1. IWWMW park across spaces? (parking-across-a space)
2. IWWMW park closer together? (parking-against-a space)
3. IWWMW rotate parking spaces? (parking-and-a space)
4. IWWMW regulate the flow of traffic? (parking-before-a space)
5. IWWMW park cars upon each other? (parking-upon-a space)
6. IWWMW shop without leaving our cars? (parking-near a space)

The leap between insertion of a relational word and development of a redefinition does not have to be logical. This technique, like most divergent thinking methods, facilitates stimulation. It cannot guarantee that you will think of a specific redefinition every time you use it. However, it is important that you write down whatever redefinitions come to mind—without evaluating them. Evaluation should be reserved for another time.

Analogies. This technique is one of the most powerful of all aids to thought stimulation. The reason is its ability to take problem solvers away from their problems. That is, analogies have the potential to allow us to develop new problem perspectives by temporarily concentrating our problem-solving efforts upon an indirectly related aspect of the general problem situation. When our efforts in suspending conscious attention allow us to view our problems as having a "life of their own" (de Bono, 1970), new perspectives will flow more readily.

The steps involved in one way of using analogies to develop new perspectives are relatively simple:

1. Generate a list of things similar to your initial problem statement.
2. Select one of these analogies. Base your selection upon the degree to which an analogy appears to be unrelated to your initial definition. Also, try to use animate analogies to deal with inanimate problems and vice versa.
3. Describe and elaborate upon your selected analogy in as much detail as possible. Try to use many descriptions which imply or involve action.
4. Examine each description and elaboration and use them as stimuli to suggest redefinitions.
5. If necessary, select another analogy and repeat steps 3 and 4.

To illustrate this method, consider the following problem: IWWMW encourage people to use their seatbelts while driving? Analogies to this problem can be generated by saying, "Encouraging people to use their seatbelts while driving is like . . .." Then, list as many analogies as you can think of. Possible analogies for this problem might include:

- ... tying down luggage on top of a car.
- ... preventing the wind from blowing down a fence.
- ... getting a hot air balloon to change directions.
- ... nailing two boards together.
- ... getting a tree to grow straight up.

Although I know very little about it, I have decided to select the analogy of getting a hot air balloon to change direction. The initial problem is primarily animate since it involves developing ways to get people to change. The analogy I have selected, in contrast, is inanimate since it involves changing an object.

What I know about this problem is:

• The wind is the primary determinant of the direction a balloon will take.

• Hot air makes a balloon rise and fall, but does not directly influence its lateral direction.

• To change a balloon's direction, you would have to overcome the force of the wind when you want to change.

• You need to decide where you want to go.

• It may be more difficult to change the direction of a heavy balloon than a light balloon.

• Assuming the direction can be controlled, a compass and visual cues from the ground can be used to keep the balloon on course.

• The force used to change direction must not be so strong as to endanger occupants of the balloon's gondola.

• There must be some way to control the force used to change direction, in order to keep the balloon on course.

After examining these descriptions, several redefinitions of the seat belt problem might be suggested. For example, some possible redefinitions might be: IWWM . . .

1. air pressure be used to hold people in their seats during accidents?

2. seats push people upward into seatbelts held in a pre-fixed position?

3. we counter arguments people use to justify not wearing seatbelts?

4. cars be started only when seat belts are fastened?

5. people decide on their own to use seatbelts?

6. we decrease the weight of seatbelts so they won't be felt by the wearer?

7. visual cues be used to motivate people to wear their seatbelts?
8. cars be made structurally safer when people wear seatbelts?
9. people be protected from injury in cars during an accident?

In looking over these redefinitions, some of them may appear to be problutions to you. If so, then you might consider implementing them as possible solutions to the problem. Otherwise, you will need to treat the redefinition as a stimulus for new redefinitions or as a problem to work on for generating ideas.

Source Searching. This technique isn't so much a specific method for developing new definitions as it is a basic mechanism for thinking about problems. Understanding problem situations involves a search for core elements underlying specific problems. We want to know what the "real" problem is. The technique of Source Searching assists in locating this problem by helping you develop redefinitions which become progressively less abstract.

The steps involved in using this approach are (Van-Gundy, 1983):

1. Begin by trying to turn your attention away from the specific problem. Try to forget the problem temporarily.
2. Think of the major principle or concept underlying the problem. Use this principle or concept to restate the problem at a fairly high level of abstraction
3. List solutions which might be used to resolve the abstract problem
4. Restate the problem at a lower level of abstraction.
5. List solutions which might be used to resolve this problem.

6. Continue developing less abstract definitions and generating solutions for each until you have exhausted all possibilities.
7. Examine all of the solutions you generated. Using them as stimuli, try to generate any redefinitions you can think of.
8. If these redefinitions seem too general, use them as stimuli to generate more specific redefinitions.
9. Select the one redefinition which best captures the essence of your problem.

To practice with this technique, you might use the problem of encouraging people to use their seatbelts. Begin by trying to forget about the specific problem of seatbelt usage. Think, instead, about the broader problem represented. In this case, you might redefine the problem as: IWWMW encourage people to change? Using this statement, you then should list possible solutions. For instance, you might think of:

- Ask them.
- Tell them.
- Pay them.
- Beg them.
- Reward them whenever they change in the desired direction.
- Show them how they would benefit by changing.
- Threaten them with punishment.
- Hypnotize them.

After generating solutions, you next should develop a less abstract statement of your original problem. For instance, you might use a problem such as: IWWMW

encourage people to be more safety conscious? Some potential solutions to this problem might be:

- Give them safety-related literature to read.
- Conduct safety demonstrations.
- Show them how they could benefit by observing safety rules.
- Use video tapes to demonstrate what happens during accidents.

- Put up posters and produce advertisements for the media.

- Reward people when they exhibit safety-conscious behaviors.

You should continue generating solutions to problem statements progressively lower in abstraction until you begin to approach the original problem. For example, the next problem redefinition in this series might be: IWWMW encourage people to protect themselves in cars? Solutions to this problem could include:

- Install airbags.

- Teach them defensive driving skills.

- Advise them to wear seat belts.

- Advise them to wear crash helmets.

- Buy cars rated high in structural integrity.

- Drive only in the daytime on limited access highways.

When you decide to stop generating solutions to your problem statements, you should start working on generating redefinitions to your original problem. To do this, examine each solution you generated and use it as a stimulus for redefinitions. Try not to judge your definitions. Rather, generate as many as you can. Then, once you have listed as many as possible, go back and evaluate them. You may even decide to modify or combine some of your redefinitions.

To illustrate this final set of activities using the example above, you might generate such redefinitions as IWWMW:

1. ask people to wear seatbelts?

2. make it illegal to not wear seatbelts while driving?

3. fine people for not wearing seatbelts?

4. encourage people to reward themselves for wearing seatbelts?

5. show people how they would benefit from wearing seatbelts?

6. punish people for not wearing seatbelts?

7. show people how they would benefit from encouraging other people to wear seatbelts?

8. make wearing seatbelts an automatic process?

9. distribute literature on the advantages of wearing seatbelts?

10. demonstrate how seatbelts can save lives?

11. dramatize the effects of not wearing seatbelts?

12. reward people for wearing seatbelts?

13. prevent people from moving during car accidents?

14. design cars to absorb most forces from an accident?

15. encourage people to take defensive driving courses?

16. encourage people to drive defensively?

17. encourage people to buy cars rated high in withstanding crashes?

18. encourage people to drive under optimal conditions?

In looking over these redefinitions, many may appear to be problutions. Others, however, may appear to be very abstract and ill-defined. If these situations exist, you might set aside the problutions and either eliminate the other redefinitions or try to refine them further.

You also might note that the differences between many of the redefinitions are subtle. At first glance, there may be no major differences. However, you should consider any difference at all to be potentially significant. Even a slight difference could allow you to think of a problution.

On the other hand, some of the redefinitions are very different from the others. For example, some focus upon getting people to wear seatbelts, while others emphasize redesigning cars or altering driving habits. All of these are new perspectives which have broadened the original problem. Any one of them could lead to one or more problutions.

Name Changing. Semantics play a major role in our lives. Whenever we assign labels or symbols to things, we alter their meaning and how we understand them. Moreover, giving something a name causes us to derive associations from the name alone. Thus, we associate circles with round things, metal with hard things, cotton with soft things, and so forth. However, the specific associations people develop may vary considerably from one person to another, depending upon a past experience with the subject.

How you define an object, person, situation, or event will influence how you react. If you define a situation as a money problem, you probably will treat it that way. There is nothing inherently "wrong" in doing this, of course. You need to categorize problems in some way to know where to search in your short- and long-term memories for solutions. There are disadvantages, however, in immediately labelling problems. If you label a problem too narrowly, you may restrict the number of possible solutions. Or, worse, you may solve the "wrong" problem. As noted earlier in this book, it usually is preferable to achieve many different problem perspectives before attempting solutions.

One way to achieve different perspectives is to experiment with a variety of labels or problem names. This can be done by substituting words or phrases in the original statement or by developing entirely new problem statements. For example, suppose your problem is: IWWMI increase my income? At a simple level, you could restate this problem in a number of ways: IWWMI increase my take-home pay? IWWMI receive more rewards for my efforts on the job? IWWMI get more special recognition? All of these provide different perspectives which could lead, directly or indirectly, to a problution.

There also is a somewhat more abstract way to rename a problem. This method requires that you completely change the content (but not necessarily the meaning) of the problem statement. The easiest way to do this is to develop titles or short descriptive phrases for the problem.

You can do this much in the same way as you might title a report or write an advertising theme. Don't be afraid to make your titles somewhat whimsical and don't be concerned if there isn't an apparent connection between your problem and a title. Thus, for the problem of increasing your income, you might think of such titles as: "Getting More Faster," "Holding On To What You Have," "Taking It With You," "Cashing In Your Chips," "You've Got It Coming To You," "Don't Give Them More Than They Deserve," and "Don't Burn More Than You Earn."

Using these titles as stimuli, you should try to develop several problem redefinitions. For this example, you might come up with such restatements as:

1. IWWMI get paid more often?
2. IWWMI save more money?
3. IWWMI spend my money more efficiently?
4. IWWMI defer my income taxes?

5. IWWMI invest my money more wisely?
6. IWWMI work less for more money?
7. IWWMI become self-employed?
8. IWWMI budget my money better?

As with the other approaches described in this chapter, you then would select a problution (if apparent to you) or the one definition which best meets your needs at the time.

He was running down a long, dark tunnel. There was no light anywhere. He just kept running and running, hoping that he wouldn't bang into something. As long as he kept a straight course, there didn't seem to be any problem. However, whenever he went a little too far to either side, his bare arms would scrape against the rough surfaces of the tunnel. The pain, however, kept throbbing in his head.

As he ran, all he could hear was the sound of his breathing. His feet were silent as they hit the floor of the tunnel, his arms quiet as they brushed the sides of his body. Then, his breathing fell silent. His legs stopped moving. He began to somersault. Over and over he went. It even was a little fun.

And then, it was over. The tunnel ended as soon as he rolled into a solid wall at the end. The darkness slowly began to lift as light filtered through the mesh net. No, it wasn't a mesh net. It was cobwebs. No, that wasn't it either. It was just sticky stuff on his eyelashes.

Forcing his eyelids open, Mike regained enough consciousness to realize that he had been "out" for quite a while. The throbbing coming from the back of his head told him that.

"It must be early evening," he thought. His watch confirmed his estimate. If he didn't hurry, he would be late for his dinner date with Mitzi.

After showering and getting dressed, Mike hurried out the door. As he jogged to his car, he knew who put him in that tunnel and caused the knot on his scalp.

Bruno was at it again. But this time, he and Mitzi were going to retaliate. Or, at least come up with a plan for a different way of dealing with Bruno.

Mike knew he just couldn't keep going on like this. He didn't want to begin wearing a helmet everyday. There had to be a better way.

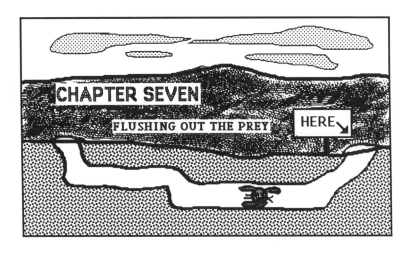

Angelo's Ristoranti was like a lot of old time, ethnic, big city eating establishments. Outside, the building had a dark brown, brick exterior constructed by immigrant workers in the 1920's. A new sign stretched across the entire facade, proudly proclaiming in neon lights: "PIZZA-SPAGHETTI-SEAFOOD." Inside, brown lattice screens with intertwining plastic vines were offset by red and white checkered table cloths. A candle adorned each table, although only a few candles were lit.

As soon as Mike entered, he noticed Mitzi sitting in a corner booth facing the door. Her eyes immediately recognized Mike and she smiled broadly. Mike walked toward her and slid into the seat facing her, his back to the front door.

"Sorry I'm late, Mitzi. I was delayed by another tap on the head. I think it was your ex-boyfriend. If this keeps up, I'm going to buy stock in an aspirin company!"

"That creep. Why doesn't he just give up and leave us alone?"

As she spoke, Mitzi's eyes narrowed and her brow wrinkled. "I'm so sick of this whole mess!"

Mike sympathized with his eyes and then replied: "Well, he's not going to go away. That's the first thing we need to realize to deal with him. We definitely need a specific plan."

After a rather heavy dinner of spaghetti and seafood, followed by thick, gooey, Italian chocolate ice cream, Mike and Mitzi began plotting. Finally, they came up with a plan satisfactory to them both. It wasn't a perfect plan, but they knew that they could make changes as they went along.

In celebration of their plan, Mike reached across the table and grabbed both of Mitzi's hands, smothering them in his. Looking deep into her eyes, he drooled: "Of all the ristoranties in the world, why did I find you in this one?"

Mitzi reeled back in muted amazement. Such a statement was so uncharacteristic of Mike. Something must have affected his thinking. It could have been the blow to his head. Or perhaps he had been watching too many old movies. It really was difficult to tell about these things.

While Mitzi pondered, Mike squeezed her hands tightly and licked the chocolate dribbling out of the corner of his mouth. He really wished he had the courage to order more ice cream.

The material presented in the previous chapters may be all you need to achieve problutions for most of your problems. However, there probably will be many situations in which you feel a need to understand a problem better. If so, you will need to analyze your problem in more depth.

Although the danger always exists that you can become too analytical in approaching problems, the benefits will outweigh the costs if a new insight is attained. Sometimes, it doesn't matter what approach you take to analyze a problem. The most important thing is that you attempt to use some process for problem analysis.

The remainder of this book deals with some general strategies and tactics you can use to "flush out a problution" and increase problem understanding. Not all of these will work for everyone in every situation. Nevertheless, they will help provide some structure for dealing with ill-structured problems.

Examining problems in depth requires a way to classify problems. There must be something concrete for you to relate to. Otherwise, one piece of structure will have no more meaning than any other. If you do not perceive anything concrete about a problem, then any relationships between pieces of structure will be equally meaningless. The pieces of structure you are aware of could remain as isolated bits of information with no apparent meaning linking them together. To solve problems, most of us need to perceive structure we can relate to.

Until then, we do not really have a problem to work on.

For instance, a manager might notice changes in the work habits of a few employees. However, unless the manager is able to relate this information to other data, such as a decline in performance or increase in an error rate, he (or she) might not perceive that a problem exists. Once a problem is perceived, the manager then must have some way of classifying it to work toward a solution. In this example, the manager could classify the situation as a performance problem, a quality control problem, an attitudinal problem, a disciplinary problem, et cetera. There even may not be one correct way to classify such situations. The point is, however, that you can't deal with a situation unless you draw some boundaries around it.

The need to classify problems is well-recognized in the literature. The behaviorist, B. F. Skinner (1953) has observed that classifying stimuli can help provide different problem perspectives. Mowrer (1960) notes that classifying makes it easier for people to relate current things to things they have experienced previously. And, classification is thought to help prevent people from inappropriately generalizing past experiences to current problem situations (Dollard & Miller, 1950). It also has been argued that classifying problems may go hand-in-hand with the process of formulating problems (D'Zurilla & Goldfried, 1971).

Information Search Strategies

The primary means used by most of us to add structure to general problem situations is to search for new information. It is only because we perceive a lack of structure in the first place that we have trouble classifying a situation as a particular type of problem. To become familiar with our problems and strive toward problutions, we need to seek all the information we can, given the constraints of the situation (e.g., time, money, personnel, perceived problem importance, et cetera).

One basic strategy for obtaining information to increase problem familiarity is to "search forward" (MacCrimmon & Taylor, 1976). This means that you start from an initial state and search for information you might use to transform the existing problem state into the goal state. According to Feldman and Kanter (1965), this procedure will be effective when the initial state is well specified and the "ratio of initial states to terminal states is small." That is, when there are few ways to describe the initial state relative to the number of goal states you might perceive.

When you understand the initial state and the ratio of initial states to goal states is large (i.e., you perceive proportionately more initial states than goal states), an alternative strategy is to work backwards in your information search. Working backwards involves starting with the goal and examining each preceding step that might have been used to reach it. Of the problems with unfamiliar initial states, this approach will work best for Type V and Type VII problems (Pure Resource and Resource/Goal problems). Working backwards would not be as effective for Type VI and Type VIII problems (Resource/Transformational and Pure Ill-structured problems), since the goal is not clearly specified in either of these problem types. That is, you need a more or less defined starting point to reach a desired goal.

Regardless of which general strategy you use, it is important that you try to add as much relevant information as you can to your perception of the situation. This information should be timely, appropriate, useful, and related to the general problem situation. All the information you collect does not have to be directly relevant to your problem. However, most of the information you use to help structure your problem obviously will have to be relevant, to solve the "right" problem. If you are trying to devise ways to reduce unemployment in your community, data on fish breeding may not be directly useful to you

(although, perhaps, it could be used to start a new industry which would help to reduce unemployment).

Search Guidelines

The general search process (either forward or backward) can be aided if you follow three basic guidelines. First, check to make sure the information you are using to define and classify your problem is valid. You don't want to try solving a Pure Goal problem that you actually perceive to be a Resource/Goal problem. For example, invalid information may lead you to believe that you are familiar with the initial state and the transformations (a Pure Goal problem). However, upon checking the validity of your information, you might find that you actually are unfamiliar with the initial state and, in fact, are dealing with a Resource/Goal problem. Once you make this check and are satisfied with your perception of the problem, you can proceed with whatever strategy you decide to use. However, if you discover that you have been viewing the problem incorrectly (for your needs), you may want to gather new information and reclassify the problem.

Determining the validity of your information can take many forms. For example, you can check some information by consulting authoritative resources such as experts in the area or reputable books and periodicals. However, when you do this you should try to determine if the information is up-to-date. Sometimes you won't have the time or opportunity to check the timeliness of information and you will have to rely upon your intuition.

A second guideline is to consider the costs of an information search. Costs can be almost anything, including money, time, people, energy, effort, et cetera. Depending upon the particular problem situation you face, any number of different factors may or may not seem important to you. However, when a factor does seem important to you, you will need to decide if the costs of acquiring a resource are likely to exceed any expected benefits. For instance, if a thorough information search will require 10 hours of your time, you must decide if the problem is worth it. If you decide it isn't, then you will need to consider the costs of conducting a shortened search or other ways of gathering information.

A third guideline is to acquire as much information as possible given the time and other resources available to you. It is far better to err on the side of too much information than too little. Once you have collected all the available information, you then can throw out that which doesn't seem useful. Deciding which information to discard may be facilitated if you first categorize the information. Categorizing information also will make it easier to refer to in the future, if necessary.

Mixed Scanning

The processes of working forward and backward can be enhanced by using an approach known as "mixed scanning" (Etzioni, 1968). According to Etzioni, mixed scanning aids in problem understanding by altering perspectives. To use mixed scanning, you should try to switch back and forth between an all-encompassing view of the problem to a more detailed subset of it. For example, I often ride a bicycle to work and must constantly focus my eyes right in front of my bike to watch for broken glass and other obstacles which can wreak havoc upon bicycle tires.

However, I also need to keep my eyes on the road ahead to avoid running into parked cars, or pedestrians walking in the street. Since both of these activities are necessary and I can't do them at the same time, I must switch back and forth rather rapidly in my scanning. As I am engaged in both of these activities, I also need to maintain awareness of where I am going and adjust my direction accordingly.

When you use mixed scanning to add information to problem situations, you constantly need to be aware of your overall perceptions of the problems. These perceptions gradually should become clearer the more you switch back and forth. The reason is that each switch may be accompanied by the acquisition of new information to help structure the problem. Eventually, a problution should emerge.

A similar situation exists when I am working on a book. I usually start out with a general idea (a broad perspec-

tive). After much thinking, I develop a rough outline (a more detailed perspective), see how the outline fits the more general idea (a broad perspective), write a rough draft of a chapter (a detailed perspective), determine how well the chapter fits the larger idea (a broad perspective), and so forth until a detailed outline for the book emerges. In practice, this process doesn't end until I have written a complete manuscript. However, the more developed the book becomes, the less need there is for me to relate each specific aspect to the larger idea.

This condition often occurs when a document almost seems to write itself. The situation is structured sufficiently so that information gathering is minimal. In contrast, what often is referred to as "writer's block" occurs when structuring needs are very high. Both situations differ primarily in their degree of familiarity to the problem solver (in this case, the writer). For this reason the first page of any writing usually is seen as the most difficult.

The same usually holds true of most problem situations. It can be very difficult to begin solving a problem, but you eventually realize that you must start somewhere and then make adjustments as you go along. The process usually becomes easier as you proceed. However, you would waste your time if you become overly concerned with deciding upon the "best" starting point. There really is no such thing.

When using mixed scanning, you probably should not spend too much time studying the problem from either a broad or a detailed perspective (Rubenstein, 1982). If you remain in a broad scan too long, you may suffer a loss of vigilance and overlook an important aspect of the problem situation; if you remain in a detailed scan too long, you might lose sight of the larger problem (the "can't-see-the-forest-for-the-trees" syndrome). Thus, a balanced amount of time in both modes would seem to be most productive.

One reason that mixed scanning may work so well could be its role in structuring ill-structured problems (ISPs) as described by Simon (1973). According to Simon, ISPs should be treated as a series of well-structured problems (WSPs). That is, ISPs can be dealt with best by treating them as sets of more manageable WSPs. Because WSPs have more perceived structure than ISPs, they are easier to deal with and understand. As noted before, Simon even goes so far to say that "there are no WSPs, only ISPs that have been formalized for problem solvers" (p. 186).

A basic process which seems to underlie mixed scanning (as well as all problem-finding activity) is the use of successive iterations or cycles (Bourne, Dominowski & Loftus, 1979). Most problems require that we take some action, evaluate the effect of the action on the problem, take any additional actions required, and so on until a satisfactory problem state is achieved. It would be extremely rare for any problem-finding activity to be completed within one cycle. It is possible that an experienced problem finder dealing with a problem of high or perhaps moderate familiarity might be able to develop a problution with only one cycle of information gathering and analysis. However, it seems more reasonable to assume that most of us will need several cycles of processing to structure our problems sufficiently (Hirschman, 1982). Because mixed scanning and treating ISPs as a series of WSPs both involve more than one cycle of activity, you should expect that most of your problem-finding activities will involve mutilple cycles.

The cyclical nature of problem finding will be more evident as you become more analytical in your information gathering activities. If you are unable to develop a problution using methods which prompt different problem perspectives (such as those in Chapters Five and Six) or general information gathering processes, you might wish to try a more specific and analytical approach. In particular, you might want to break down your problems into their major components as discussed in Chapter Three. Then, you could use these components as major reference points while you attempt to add problem structure.

As you add information to each of the three major problem components, your familiarity with the problem should increase accordingly. Each time you exceed the threshhold of familiarity (the point at which you perceive a problem component to be familiar) for a particular component, the problem type will change. For instance, you might begin with a Pure Ill-structured probelm (Type VIII), proceed to a Transformational/Goal problem (Type IV), and end up with a Well-Structured problem (Type I).

Transforming Problem Types

The remainder of this chapter will deal with transforming problems for which you are unfamiliar with either the initial or goal states. Problems with familiar initial states include: Pure Transformational problems (Type II), Pure Goal Problems (Type III), and Transformational/Goal problems (Type IV). Well-Structured problems (Type I) depicted in **Table 3-1** also are included in this category, but will not be considered here since they are problutions. When you perceive the initial problem state to be unfamiliar, the available problem types include: Pure Resource problems (Type V), Resource/Transformational problems (Type VI), Resource/Goal problems (Type VII), and Pure Ill-Structured problems (Type VIII).

For many situations, the logical starting point for problems with an unfamiliar initial state (Types V, VI, VII, and VIII) will be the initial state. This is because: "If you don't know where you are, you're not likely to know how to get to where you want to go." For instance, if you find yourself somewhere on a remote stretch of highway in Texas and you want to go to Dallas, it will be very difficult for you to get there if you don't know where you are in Texas. (This obviously assumes that you already have dealt with the problem of deciding where you want to go—Type V and VI problems would apply in this example). Any direction and any road will be equally useful to you in such a situation. However, this will not always be the case, since there will be many situations in which you may feel more comfortable starting with the goal state.

On the surface, such a philosophy seems to suggest that you initially should deal with these problems using a "working forward" search. However, remember that you may have to deal with many subproblems that are well-structured. To deal with these, you may have to work either forward, backward, or both, depending upon your ability to acquire information and your overall understanding of the problem situation. (i.e., some subproblems may have either well-defined initial or goal states).

The basic problem-finding approach for dealing with problem types II through VIII can be illustrated using the flowchart shown in **Figure 7-1.** As shown in this figure, you should begin by determining if the initial state is familiar to you. If not, you should identify and acquire resources you need to clarify the initial state. If you are familiar with the initial state, then you should identify and specify goal states. You probably will need to use several cycles of information gathering for either of these states to become familiar to you.

Once resources are acquired to clarify the initial state, the problem should be transformed into a type I, II, III, or IV problem, depending upon the nature of the problem at the outset. For example, defining the initial state of a Resource/Transformational problem (Type VI) would result in a Pure Transformational problem (Type II). An example of such an operation is shown in **Figure 7-2.** In this figure, information is gathered to make the initial state more like the goal state. Once this is accomplished, all that remains is to develop transformations (i.e., generate ideas) to close the gap between the two states. An example of the situation depicted in **Figure 7-2** would be the design of a totally new product to solve a problem not solved by any product currently on the market. Clarifying the initial states of Type V, VII, and VIII problems would result in Type I, III, and IV problems, respectively.

If you clarify your problem's initial state and produce a Pure Goal (Type III) or Transformational/Goal problem (Type IV), you next should try to identify and specify the goal state. As shown in **Figure 7-1,** doing this should result in a Well-Structured (Type I) or Pure Transformational problem (Type II). If it is a Type I problem, you can terminate the process; if you end up with a Type II problem, then you will need to generate solutions to close the gap

Figure 7-1. Decision flow chart for developing problutions.

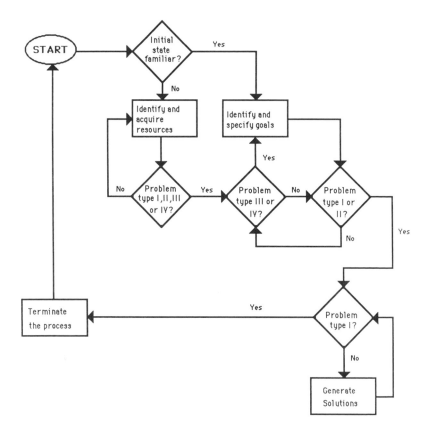

between the states. Closing the gap between the initial and goals states is, of course, your overall objective. You eventually want to develop a problution. At this point, you should be able to terminate the process or you will need to continue generating solutions until a problution is produced.

Note that when you begin with a problem for which you are familiar with the intial state, less time and effort usually will be required than when you are unfamiliar with one or more states. When you initially perceive a situation to be a Pure Goal (Type III) or Transformational/Goal problem (Type IV), you can devote your time to clarifying the goal state, since the initial state already should be familiar to you. Of course, dealing with a Pure Transformational problem would be even easier, since all you need to do is develop transformations to close the gap between the states.

Figure 7-1 illustrates the general operations needed to deal with the major types of ill-structured problems. It should be apparent that flow charts can simplify what may be a very complex process. Converting any problem from one type to another can be easier said than done.

Figure 7-2. Effects of acquiring resources for a Type VI problem.

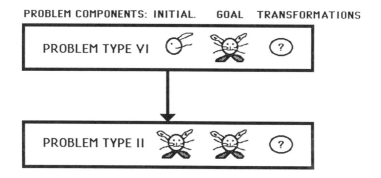

PROBLEM COMPONENTS: INITIAL. GOAL TRANSFORMATIONS

PROBLEM TYPE VI

PROBLEM TYPE II

It usually is not enough just to say that you should acquire resources and alter the problem to make it more familiar to you. There are many situations in which you will need to have more specific guidance. For these situations, you may want to have more refined approaches for each problem type. These are discussed in the next chapter.

Mike decided it was time for them to leave. The flickering of the melting candle on their table told him that Angelo's would be closing soon. Besides, there still was a lot he wanted to talk over with Mitzi. While wiping the chocolate from the corner of his mouth, Mike smoothly stood up, walked around to Mitzi's chair, and helped her up.

As she was standing up, Mitzi tried to glance into Mike's eyes without him noticing. What she saw worried her. Mike's eyes seemed to be almost glazed over. The quivering life she had noticed before was lacking. His eyes now seemed to be those of a robot. The shimmering brown pools she had come to adore now appeared stagnant.

Mike paid the bill and his respects to Angelo, the proprietor. He then guided Mitzi through the front door and out onto the sidewalk. While walking, they began to discuss ways to get Bruno. By encouraging the other person and listening carefully, they came up with almost 25 ideas in less than ten minutes. Mitzi noticed, however, that Mike's eyes remained the same—unwavering and somewhat distant.

Just as they were about to round a corner, a white van came screeching by. It shot through a large, brown puddle next to the curb where Mike and Mitzi were walking. Mike grabbed Mitzi and quickly pulled her down and away from the curb. A shot suddenly rang out and a bullet splintered the bricks just above their heads, missing them by only centimeters. For Mike, however, the worst part of the incident was the brown mud splattered all over his white suit.

Bruno apparently had struck again, thought Mike. But he didn't want to say anything to Mitzi and worry her unnecessarily. The poor kid had been through enough already. He decided, instead, to divert her attention.

While she was still in his grasp, he pulled her close and kissed her hard on the mouth. She responded by rubbing her hands in the mud on his suit. She used small circular movements, offset occasionally by an eliptical movement. Mike knew he was in for a large dry cleaning bill, but he didn't care. It would be worth it!

CHAPTER EIGHT

TRANSFORMATIONS

A speeding car suddenly rounded the corner where Mike and Mitzi were embracing. As the car hit the puddle near the curb, a wave of cold water washed over them, cooling their passion. Shaking off the moisture, they stood up and began walking down the street as if nothing had happened.

Mitzi, however, was still shaken from the near miss of the bullet. And, she still was worried about Mike. He definitely had been acting rather strangely lately. At that moment, Mike gave her shoulder a little squeeze and she became lost in her thoughts about Bruno and her relationship with Mike.

They soon reached Mike's apartment and Mike ushered Mitzi in through the front door. He offered her a seat on his couch and a candy bar. Although there was nothing unusual about his offer of a candy bar, Mike's robot-like tone of voice was quite disconcerting. Upon hearing him speak, Mitzi stiffened slightly and then relaxed just enough to politely refuse. She sensed something was wrong with Mike. However, he apparently had not noticed her reaction. He almost didn't seem to care. In fact, his only visible response was to spin on his heels and walk purposively toward his kitchen.

After about five minutes, Mike reappeared. He seemed to stagger toward Mitzi. He walked around behind where she was sitting and placed both of his hands around her neck. She felt his breath against the back of her head. Then, she smelled his breath. There was something odd about it. It definitely wasn't alcohol. Yet, it had a distinctive odor.

Mike's hands slowly began to squeeze Mitzi's neck. His breathing was labored as he pressed ever tighter. Mitzi became faint. She was to the point of blacking out when she recognized the smell on Mike's breath. It was a carefully blended, medium-brown, semi-sweet, Swiss chocolate. And then, just before lapsing into a forced

slumber, she heard Mike's voice:
"It's O.K. Bruno. You don't need to worry anymore. Everything is under control. The chocolate is ours and we'll never have to share again!"

Chapter Seven discussed general strategies for developing problutions when initially dealing with ill-structured types of problems. The basic procedures for doing this involved working forward or backward from different problem states. For some problem situations, however, you may need more specific procedures.

One way to make a more detailed analysis of problem transformations is to start by classifying your problem according to one of the problem types shown in **Table 3-1.** Since each problem type has a different degree of familiarity, you will need to approach each problem a little differently. For example, you will need to deal differently with problems with a familiar initial state than with problems with an unfamiliar initial state. Typically, you first should deal with each unfamiliar problem component and attempt to transform it into a more familiar component. Depending upon the type of problem you begin with, any number of operations may be needed to produce a problution or Type I problem.

In the remainder of this chapter I will discuss ways to deal with specific problem types. Problem Types V through VIII will be dealt with first since they require the most structuring (i.e., they have the greatest number of unfamiliar states.) Moreover, all the initial states of these types are unfamiliar. These are the problem states which usually need to be clarified before dealing with goal states or transformations. Problem Types IV through II then will be discussed as the final stages of problution development.

Initial   Goal   Transformations

Pure Resource Problems (Type V). When you initially perceive a situation to be a Type V problem, you have drawn three conclusions about the situation: (1) You are familiar with the goal you want to achieve, (2) you have at least an approximate idea of how to achieve the goal (i.e., make the necessary transformations), and (3) you are unfamiliar with where you are (i.e., you are uncertain about the exact nature of the initial state). Three examples of such problems would be:

1. You are lost in a big city and are trying to return to your hotel. You are familiar with the types of transportation available in this city and how to obtain them. You also know the address of your hotel and a few major landmarks near it. However, you are unfamiliar with your present location. You don't know where you are.

2. You are the manager of a nonprofit, social service agency. You and your board of directors decide you need additional funding for the agency to purchase some important equipment. You know how much money you will need to buy the equipment (the goal state). Unfortunately, the accounting procedures you have been using don't allow you to determine accurately how much money you cur-

rently have available (the initial state). You have a rough idea about how much money is available. Nevertheless, you need more information to reliably estimate the amount of additional funds you will need. It is not likely that the amount currently budgeted for such equipment will be sufficient. Because of your experience with similar problems in the past, you are familiar with several ways to seek additional funds.

3. You have been hired to assist a consultant for a large organization. You are told that your task is to conduct an employee training program to improve interdepartmental communication. The consultant tells you what the communication between departments should be like after the training program. She also provides a detailed outline for you to follow in conducting your workshops. However, you are given no information on the present state of interdepartmental communications. All you know is that someone has perceived a problem to exist and now you are involved.

These examples represent somewhat different types of pure resource problems. In each case, the primary task facing the problem finder is to acquire information to clarify the initial state. Once this is done, a problution should exist. Increasing your familiarity with the initial state of a Type V problem automatically will lead to a Type I problem as long as the other problem components remain constant (as you perceive them).

The amount of information available about the states and transformations of any problem usually will vary from one situation to another. In addition, the best approach for dealing with different situations also may vary. It is up to you, the problem finder, to decide upon the best approach.

According to Grandori (1984), most people use random search strategies to deal with what we refer to as Type V problems. Faced with an unlimited set of initial state possibilities, problem finders select actions based upon the order in which they encounter them. That is, they test the first bit of information they come upon and see how it might affect their problem. Quite often, the initial state selected is simply a matter of timing. We define the initial state using information in the order in which we acquire it. It must be noted, however, that these strategies represent a descriptive approach to problem finding. We are more concerned here with prescriptive approaches.

In the first example, the problem finder needs to determine where he is before he can return to the hotel. To do this, he might begin walking (or use other transportation known to him) in the direction in which he believes the hotel is located. As he travels, he may recognize familiar sights which he can use to correct his path if necessary.

In the second example, the problem finder obviously needs to gather more reliable data about currently available funds to determine how much additional funding will be needed. To make this determination, he could locate the most recent budgetary information. Then, he might try to determine each preceding budget state by analyzing expenditures and verifying their validity. Eventually, he may be able to trace the problem back to an unrecorded expenditure or some other bit of information that would help clarify the current budget state.

Finally, in the third example, the problem finder is faced with what might be perceived to be a frustrating, lose-lose situation. If she follows the outline and is successful in achieving the desired state, she never will know if the change was due to her program. It would be quite possible that the program had no effect and what she measured actually was the current state of communications (thus indicating a likely misdiagnosis of the problem). If she follows the outline and is not successful in achieving the goals given her, her program may be blamed. She could be held responsible for not achieving her goals, even though it is possible that the outcomes she did achieve represented a substantial improvement over the original situation. Thus, the problem finder would be well advised to try and specify the current problem state. To do this, she might interview a sample of employees from each department and then categorize the information in some useful way.

In all of these examples, you could collect information and transform the problems by working either forward or backward. As noted earlier, the choice of either approach depends upon a number of factors, such as how familiar you are with the problem states. In fact, familiarity with the states will be a major determining factor.

For Type V problems, working backwards would seem to be a logical approach for many situations. Since you are familiar with the goal and the operations needed to achieve it, it should be relatively easy to move backwards from the goal, toward an initial state. As you make each move toward the initial state, you sometimes can observe what move came before it, and so forth, until you reach a satisfactory initial state. If, however, you are not familiar with the goal state (such as is the case with problem types VII and VIII), working forward might be more appropriate, once you have settled on a tentative initial state. Working backwards also might be difficult when you have insufficient or unreliable information.

One general method of working forward is known as means-ends analysis. As described by Newell and Simon (1972), means-ends analysis is used by comparing differences between initial and goal states, determining if a discrepancy exists between the states, and then applying some means (or "operator") to resolve the discrepancy. This process is repeated until you no longer perceive a discrepancy to exist. It also would be possible to work backwards using means-ends analysis if you redefined your initial and goal states.

In the research on means-ends analysis using con-

Great Works

A MEAN END

RUNNING TOWARD A GOAL

trived problems, it has been found that novice problem solvers tend to employ means-ends analysis more often than expert problem solvers (Larkin, McDermott, Simon & Simon, 1980). In one experimental study, Sweller (1983) observed that subjects generated moves using the problem state attained, rather than the goal, when they had learned a specific way of responding to similar problems. That is, when they acquired what Sweller referred to as a "learned construct," they used the current problem state as the basis for additional action instead of the goal state as is used in means-ends analysis. Apparently, acquisition of this "learned construct" was sufficient to allow the subjects in his study to operate more as experts than as novices. It should be noted, however, that the problems in this study were artificial in content (i.e., contrived).

On the surface, these studies appear to be based upon different types of problems than those dealt with here. Research on means-ends analysis usually involves problems in which the initial and goal states are familiar to the problem solver—in other words, more or less well-structured types of problems. However, since most problem finders are faced continuously with a well-structured problem (Simon, 1973), means-ends analysis also will be applicable to most ill-structured problems.

Sweller and Levine (1982) note that means-ends analysis is more likely to be used if the goal is specified clearly. Of the problem types considered here, that would mean you would be more likely to try means-ends analysis for Pure Transformational, Pure Resource, and Resource/Transformational Problems (Types II, V and VI). The goals of these problems are familiar to the problem finder. However, as noted above, it also is possible to use means-ends analysis with other types of problems. Goal familiarity will be discussed in more detail later in this chapter.

Generally speaking, it would seem logical to work forwards or backwards from the goal when dealing with Type V problems. There also may be situations in which you might be successful by working in relation to familiar transformations (characteristic of Pure Goal, Pure Resource, and Resource/Goal problems) rather than goal states. For example, in one of the problem examples described previously, the situation involves returning to your hotel when you don't know where you are. However, you are familiar with available means of transportation (the known transformation alternatives). To deal with this situation, you might try working backwards from the hotel and retrace your movements to your current position. On the other hand, you also might try working either forwards or backwards using the potential transportation transformations as a subgoal. Thus, you might locate a nearby bus stop and seek information about bus routes which could take you within walking distance of your hotel (working forwards).

Technically speaking, such an approach could be viewed as another form of means-ends analysis. Whether it is or not probably is irrelevant, since it at least provides you with another way to deal with your problems. The important point is that you should use the components of your problems as reference points from which you can work forwards or backwards to acquire information and increase your familiarity with the components.

Initial　　　　Goal　　　　Transformations

Resource/Transformational Problems (Type VI). Problems you initially categorize as Resource/Transformational will be viewed by you as having: (1) an unfamiliar initial state, (2) a familiar goal state, and (3) unfamilar transformation (i.e., you are uncertain about how to close the gap between the states). In other words, you know where you want to go, but you don't know where you are or how to get to your goal. The primary difference between this type of problem and Pure Resource problems (Type V) is that Type VI problems have unfamiliar transformations.

Using the same situations used to illustrate Type V problems, three examples of Resource/Transformational problems would be:

1. You are lost in a big city and trying to return to your hotel. You are familiar with the hotel's location (a familiar goal state). Unfortunately, you are unfamiliar with available transportation (other than walking, of course) and you have relatively little idea about where you are now (an unfamiliar initial state).

2. As the manager of a nonprofit social service agency faced with the need for additional funding to purchase equipment, you know exactly how much money you need. However, due to unreliable accounting procedures, you are unfamiliar with the amount of existing funds. To make matters worse, you lack experience in acquiring funds and are unfamiliar with any reliable procedures.

3. A consultant has hired you to assist in conducting a training program to improve interdepartmental communications within an organization. The good news is that she has told you what communications should be like after the training program; the bad news is that she has given you no information on the current state of interdepartmental communications. Moreover, it is up to you to decide how to conduct the program. The consultant has not given you any idea about what type of program to conduct and you have little experience with such programs.

Unlike Type V problems where your primary task is to clarify the initial state of your problem, Type VI problems require that you also develop transformations. You must make the initial state like the goal state. To do this, you will need to generate a number of different potential transformations.

You first will need to collect information to make the initial state familiar, just as you would with a Type V problem. However, you now will have to go one step further and develop transformations. The reason for this is that once the initial state is familiar, you will be dealing with a Type II problem (Pure Transformational). Type II problems have familiar initial and goal states, but require transformations to change them into problutions.

In the first example, the problem finder should gather information about his present location. He can do this in the same manner suggested for a Type V problem—walking in what he believes is the correct direction and readjusting the path based upon landmarks or information gathered from passersby. Once he or she is satisfied with his knowledge of the present location, he can begin to explore available transportation.

In the second example, the problem finder will need to begin by increasing the reliability of information about the current financial situation. Following this, he or she will need to learn how to acquire additional funds. In this instance, he could temporarily delegate part of the problem to someone else with more expertise in fund acquisition. One possibility might be someone more knowledgeable about the politics of internal fund raising in the organization. On the other hand, he or she may decide to retain direct control over the problem and seek the information alone.

Finally, in the third example, the problem finder needs to start by becoming informed about the current state of interdepartmental communications. Then, she will need to educate herself about programs with the potential to deal with the situation. Again, she could delegate this responsibility or assume it herself. In either case, she will need to generate and then select the best way to make the current state of communications more like the desired state.

Initial   Goal   Transformations

Resource/Goal Problems (Type VII). Type V and Type VI problems are very similar in that both have unfamiliar initial states and familiar goal states. The only difference between them is familiarity with the transformations. Resource/Goal and Pure Ill-Structured problems (Types VII and VIII) are related in a similar way in that they differ only in familiarity with the transformations. Resource/Goal problems, in particular, are characterized by: (1) an unfamiliar initial state, (2) an unfamiliar goal state, and (3) familiar transformations. In essence, you don't know where you are or where you want to go, but you know some solutions nevertheless.

In the academic literature, such situations are very similar to what has been referred to as the "garbage can" model of organizational choice (Cohen, March & Olsen, 1972). One part of this model involves the concept of solutions in search of problems. Great discoveries and inventions which occur due to serendipity often fall into this category. For example, Post-It™ notes started out as a byproduct. They evolved because a glue developed by the 3M Company was judged (at that time) to be inferior. It had only marginally effective adhesive properties. However, a 3M employee was looking for a way to mark songs in his church hymnal without having slips of paper continuously falling out. The glue (a solution) was matched with the problem and Post-It™ notes were born (although not without much work to get them to market).

I have at least two solutions in search of problems in my office right now. Both of these were sent to me by inventors who asked me to help them find problems

Chef Gel prepares a meal
in search of a
customer

to which their solutions could be applied. Originally, each of these inventions was designed as a solution to a specific problem. (One was designed as quick-release dog leash and the other as a toy to entertain house cats.)

However, both inventors eventually decided they needed a more expanded market. (Don't ask why inventors of animal products seem to seek me out!)

Other instances of Resource/Goal problems can be illustrated using the three examples discussed previously:

1. You are lost in the big city and you don't know where you are or where your hotel is located. You are, however, familiar with types of transportation available in this city.

2. You are the social service agency manager who needs to obtain additional funds to purchase some equipment. You don't know how much money you have now or how much more money you will need. You do know how to go about obtaining additional funds.

3. You have been hired to assist a consultant in developing a training program to improve interdepartmental communications in an organization. You are given no information about either the current or desired states of communication. However, you are very skilled and experienced at developing communication skills workshops.

Dealing with these three problems could involve quite different approaches from those used with problem Types V and VI (Pure Resource and Resource/Transformational problems). To deal with Type VII problems, you must become familiar with both the initial and goal states. However, since you are familiar with transformations, it would appear that you will not need to bother with them.

In some situations this may be true. However, there may be many occasions in which your familiarity with transformations may be a distinct disadvantage. Being familiar with transformations may act as a perceptual block and prevent you from exploring other alternatives. Or, it may cause you to restrict your search for solutions to a limited area. For instance, the solution of a quick-release dog leash may cause you to narrow your problem searching to areas involving animal restraints. In fact, what you really might want to do is search for problems which could be solved using the basic principle underlying the leash's design. That is, instead of viewing the leash as an animal restraint, try to look at it as a general quick-release restraint mechanism applicable to many problems.

The communication training program problem could be used as another example of this dilemma. You might decide to use an "off-the-shelf" training program (a familiar transformation). However, after you begin the program, you might discover that the "real" problem (in terms of the initial and goal states) is not communication between departments, but role clarity within departments. Thus, in this instance, your familiar transformation would not be useful if you clarify the problem states in terms of how well people understand their jobs. As a result, the transformation you might need could involve individual coaching of employees or training in basic job performance skills. The lesson, then, is to be cautious before jumping to conclusions about either problems or solutions.

The difficulties created by an unfamiliar goal state have been recognized in the research literature. For instance, Greeno (1976) has observed that people faced with indefinite goals often search for and collect information without knowing how the information might be used. Such behavior contrasts with actions often used to deal with more structured problems. For these problems, any information collected usually will be assessed for its usefulness in achieving a defined goal state. That is, the information is sought with a specific purpose in mind.

One general strategy for dealing with Type VII problems is to first collect information about the initial state and then the goal state. Once these states are clarified satisfactorily, you then should evaluate how likely it is that known transformations will be capable of closing the gap between the states. If the solutions known to you do not seem capable of producing a problution, you will need to generate additional solutions and evaluate their usefulness.

To become familiar with the initial state, you could use whatever information is available to clarify the initial state. If this doesn't work, you could try working backwards from known transformations. Working backwards in such a situation can be illustrated using the previous example of the interdepartmental communications training program. A possible known transformation in this instance might be an existing communication skills training design. Using the topical areas contained within this design, you might develop a questionnaire to evaluate the employees' perceptions about the current state of interdepartmental communications.

Thus, you would move from a solution in one situation to an initial problem state in another situation. Although such a procedure might not be technically "correct" as a means for working backwards, its utility as a method for clarifying a problem state is more important. In other words, "if it works for you, use it."

Once you have become familiar with the initial state, your problem situation will be converted to a Type III, Pure Goal problem. For this type of problem, a problution often will emerge once you become familiar with your goal. However, when goal specification is your primary task, you should concentrate on developing a variety of realistic goals from which you can select the best one. It is important that your goals be optimal (Simon, 1955). If your aspirations are too high, you are likely to end up frustrated; if they are too low, your motivation to deal with the problem may decline.

If you are unable to acquire information about the goal state by simple search methods, you can try an incremental strategy such as "disjointed incrementalism (Braybrooke & Lindblom, 1963). The basic procedure involved in incrementalism is to take only small steps from the initial state toward the goal state. In doing this, you should concentrate upon differences between consequences of the initial state and consequences of other possible initial states. When a difference is evident to you, you will need to decide how much of one initial state may be worth sacrificing or trading off to achieve another initial state. If you continue in this activity long enough, you gradually should achieve a desired goal state or problution.

As a simple illustration, consider the previous problem of being lost in the big city. Each time you make a move in such a situation, you would be altering your initial problem state. Using an incremental strategy, you would need to determine the cost of taking one move versus another. Thus, you might be standing on a street corner faced with the option of going right or left. If you go left and it turns out to be an incorrect move, you may decide you will have farther to walk to return to your original location than had you gone right. However, if you turn left and it turns out to be a correct move, you will be closer to your objective of the hotel.

After a series of such moves and decisions, you should be closer to your goal than had you made more random moves. Moreover, you do not have to deal with the problem of evaluating a long list of alternatives. In incrementalism, you base each succeeding move on the previous one. Thus, your goal does not need to be as well specified as may be the case with many other approaches (Taylor, 1974).

| Initial | Goal | Transformations |

Pure III-Structured Problems (Type VIII). Many of the world's most pressing and important problmes fall into this category. In contrast to all other problem types, Pure III-structured problems are characterized by a com-

plete lack of familiarity with any of the problem components. When faced with this type of problem, you are
unfamiliar with the initial state, the goal state, and any
potential transformations. You do not know where you
are, where you want to go, or how to get there. In other
words, you are faced with a "mess."

Admittedly, the degree to which Type VIII problems
are familiar to you can vary across different problem
situations. More than likely, you will be partially familiar
with one or more components of most Type VIII problems.
Thus, Pure Ill-Structured problems probably are rather
rare. Nevertheless, the typical Type VIII problem represents an ambiguous, uncertain situation which you will
need to deal with by systematically increasing your familiarity with the problem components. In effect, you will
need to invent a problem and develop a problution for it.

Using the three examples described previously, Type
VIII problems can be described in the following manner:

1. You are lost in the big city. You have little or no
idea as to where you are, where your hotel is located,
and you are ignorant of available means of transportation.

2. As the manager of a social service agency, you
need to acquire funds to purchase some important equipment. Unfortunately, you don't know how much money
you have now, how much additional money you will need
to purchase the equipment, and you lack knowledge about
the appropriate procedures for obtaining funds.

3. After being hired by a consultant to assist in im-
proving interdepartmental communications, you find you
have very little information to begin doing your job. You
are not informed about either the current or desired
state of communications. To make matters worse, you
have very little knowledge about conducting training programs in this area.

In all of these examples, the problem finder must
start from "scratch" to develop a problution. Because
you may not be familiar with the parts of a Type VIII

problem, some of the general strategies discussed previously might not be effective. That is, these types of problems may be so difficult to deal with that you might need to seek ways to achieve a broader perspective. If so, many of the techniques discussed in Chapters Five and Six might be helpful. (The "Why" method might be especially useful for initially dealing with Type VIII problems.) However, if you feel fairly comfortable about dealing with a particular Type VIII problem, then you could try some of the general strategies dealt with in Chapter Seven and this chapter.

One general approach for dealing with ill-structured problems is to begin by clarifying the initial state, then the goal state and, finally, the transformations needed to close the gap between the states. The specifics involved in doing this already have been discussed in this chapter and will not be repeated here.

It should be reiterated, however, that problems you first perceive as having unfamiliar initial and goal states may require considerably more effort in defining the states than problems in which you are familiar with one of the states at the outset. For Type VIII problems, you may need to evaluate many different combinations of initial and goal states. Other problem types, in contrast, come partially constructed in the sense that at least one of the components is familiar. Whenever at least one problem component is familiar, it can be used as a fairly stable (at least in terms of your own perceptions) reference point for constructing the remaining components. As a result, your problem-finding task will be simplified somewhat.

Initial   Goal   Transformations

Transformational/Goal Problems (Type IV). Type IV problems are characterized by familiarity with the initial state. When faced with this type of problem, you know where you are. However, you need to clarify your goal state and then develop transformations to reduce the gap between the two states. That is, you know where you are, but you don't know where you want to go or how to get there.

The three basic problem examples dealt with previously can be viewed as Type IV problems if described as follows:

1. You find yourself lost in the city and unfamiliar with available transportation. Although you don't know where your hotel is located, you are familiar with where you are now.

2. Remember the manager of the social service agency? Well, you now find yourself unacquainted with how much money you need to purchase some important equipment and how to go about acquiring additional funds. The good news is that you have a pretty good idea about how much money you have now.

3. As a consultant hired to help in designing a communications skills training program, you find you are well aware of the current state of interdepartmental communications. However, you have little to go on in regard to desired communications skills. Moreover, you are inexperienced in designing training programs which might help with this problem.

To deal with these situations, you should begin by clarifying your goal state. This can be accomplished by working forward or backward as discussed in previous sections of this chapter. Once you have collected enough information to understand what you would like to achieve, you then can begin work on transformations. As noted previously, developing transformations involves generating alternatives which might help reduce the gap between the states.

Initial   Goal   Transformations

Pure Goal Problems (Type III). Problems in this category may be relatively rare, because of the somewhat odd combination of a known initial state and transformations, but an unknown goal state. As with Pure Resource (Type V) and Resource/Goal (Type VII) problems, transformations often are not available or cannot be developed until after both problem states are familiar. Of course, this will not always be true. There will be many situations in which you have solutions available to you, but remain unfamiliar with either an initial or goal state.

When trying to resolve Pure Goal problems, you need to become familiar with the goal state to develop a problution (which would be the situation created after you become familiar with the goal). However, once you have produced a problution, you may find that the transformations you initially perceived as familiar are no longer valid. (If this occurs, you will be confronted with a Type II, Pure Transformational problem.) It is important that you don't allow known transformations to influence your efforts to clarify the goal state. You should be guided by what you need to achieve and not by whatever transformations may be known to you at the time. When your problem-solving actions are guided by previously learned solutions, it is referred to as "reproductive problem solving;" when you use elements which are unfamiliar to you (such as one of the problem components), you are using "productive problem solving" (Maier, 1931).

The potentially distracting effects of known transformations can be illustrated using the three problem situations presented earlier. For Pure Goal problems, these situations can be described as follows:

1. You are lost in the big city without any knowledge of the location of your hotel. Fortunately, you are familiar with your present location and available transportation.

2. As a social service agency manager, you know how to obtain funds needed to purchase some important equipment. You also know how much money currently is

available, but you don't know how much additional money you will need to purchase the equipment.

3. As an experienced and knowledgeable trainer, you are familiar with the existing level of interdepartmental communications in the organization you have been hired to assist. However, you have very little information about the desired level of communications.

As noted above, being familiar with potential transformations for Type III problems may influence you inappropriately when you try to increase your familiarity with the goal state. For instance, in the third problem situation discussed, you might be influenced unduly by your general knowledge of training problems when you attempt to determine the communications goal state in the organization. You might try to persuade organizational members to adopt your goals (or goals of other organizations known to you) rather than have them struggle with developing their own goals. Thus, you might use reproductive problem solving and base your perceptions of where the organization should be upon solutions known to you.

It will not always be easy to overcome the potentially distracting effects of known transformations upon familiarity with either of the problem states. When one of the states is known to you, you might be able to avoid this distracting effect by limiting your information search to working either forward or backward from the remaining known state. In any event, you may want to defer thinking about transformations whenever your perception of the problem states is likely to be affected negatively.

Initial

Goal

Transformations

Pure Transformational Problems (Type II). The last category of problems to be discussed here includes situations which may be the easiest to resolve. This may not be true of all Type II problems, but it generally will be when this type is compared to the other problem types. Faced with a known initial state and a known goal state, dealing with Pure Transformational problems involves generating transformations to close the gap between the states. Using individual or group brainstorming procedures (or variations), you normally will need to develop a list of as many transformational solutions as you can think of. When doing this, it is important that you withhold all judgment. Evaluate your potential transformations only after you have listed as many as you can.

Using the problem situations dealt with previously, Type II problems can be described as follows:

1. You are wandering around in the big city. You are familiar with your present location and you know the location of your hotel. However, you have no information on available transportation.

2. As manager of a social service agency needing additional funds to purchase equipment, you are aware of how much money you have and how much you need. The only information you lack is how to go about acquiring the funds you need.

3. Asked to assist a consultant in designing a program to improve interdepartmental communications, you find that you are familiar with both the current and goal states of communications. You lack information, however, in how to design a training program capable of reducing the gap between the two states.

As noted above, dealing with these situations involves developing a number of different transformations with the potential to reduce or close the gap between initial and goal states. For some Pure Transformational Problems, the best possible transformation will be readily apparent to you. After inspecting the situation, you may be able to think of a relatively routine response that can lead to a problution. In other situations, however, you may not be quite so knowledgeable or experienced with the problem components (although you still could be familiar with them). In these situations, you probably will have to experiment with a number of different transformation possibilities.

In the examples above, the problem finder faced with obtaining additional funds may experience little difficulty in acquiring the money if familiar with the procedures involved in the organization. The consultant in the second example, however, might experience more difficulty in developing transformations if generally unfamiliar with the type of training programs needed to deal with the particular situation.

Since it is possible that your perceptions of the states may change at any time, you may need to discard or (hold in reserve) any transformations you previously generated. In such cases, your problem may need to be re-classified and dealt with accordingly. Thus, if the consultant should find that the problem is redefined as a motivational one (or redefines it), he or she will first need to become familiar with the initial or goal states (if necessary). Only then can he or she begin to generate transformations.

When her eyes first opened, all Mitzi could see was a brown haze. Mike was nowhere to be seen. She rubbed her eyes, massaged her sore neck, and walked to the bathroom to wash her face. Upon returning to Mike's living room, Mitzi once again detected the distinctive odor of a fine, medium-brown, semi-sweet, Swiss chocolate. Her nose led her to the kitchen where she saw Mike standing over a pot on the stove. He was pouring chocolate into molds. Mitzi cleared her throat and caught his attention.

"What are you doing, Mike? What's going on here? Why did you choke me into unconsciousness? Don't you like me? Why won't you answer me?"

"Questions, questions, questions. That's all you ever ask me," said Mike wiping the chocolate dripping down from the corner of his mouth. "Why don't you ask me instead about Bruno? He's the one we should be concerned about."

"O.K. I will," retorted Mitzi. "Tell me about Bruno. What's he have to do with anything?"

"He has a lot to do with everything," Mike snapped right back. "You see Mitzi, Bruno exists and he doesn't exist. He has been stalking us and we have been stalking him. However, no one has really been after anyone else. Yet, we have been both chaser and chased!"

Some brown foam began to trickle out of Mike's mouth and then his nose. He shook his head as if to clear his thoughts and his face. He then sat down on a kitchen chair. Mitzi's eyes intently followed his every move. Her eyes also began to show great compassion for the big lug. Although he didn't make much sense, she still cared for him.

Mike shoved back his chair, stood up and began pacing. Still dribbling from his mouth, he resumed speaking to Mitzi.

"What you need to understand Mitz, 'ole girl, is that I am Bruno and Bruno is I. We are one and the same . . . physically, spiritually, mentally, emotionally—however you want to wrap it. Whatever has happened to you and to me in regard to Bruno has been my doing. A long time ago, I transformed myself into Bruno. I became Bruno in my imagination and in my behavior. The only thing I had to fear from Bruno was myself. The only thing you have to fear about me is me; and you about you. I am my problem and yours."

"Whenever I have a problem, Bruno has a problem. You have a problem with Bruno only because you think you have a problem, not because Bruno is a problem to you. And, the only way you and I can get rid of Bruno is to begin viewing him as a solution. Only Bruno can solve the problem of Bruno."

Up to this point, Mitzi had been listening calmly to Mike. When he finished talking, she walked to the pot on the stove, scooped out a large spoonful and dumped it on Mike's head. Then, she licked the spoon clean and walked out of the apartment into the bright sunlight.

Someone was waiting for her on the corner. As she walked closer, she could begin to discern facial features. There was no doubt about it. Waiting for her, on the corner, was Bruno. The chase had just begun.

CHAPTER NINE

AFTER THE HUNT

The hunt is over now. You have stalked the wild solution and caught it. Victory is yours and to you go the spoils. Now is the time to sit back and relax with a favorite drink and bask in your success. You have triumphed over often impossible odds and won. Or have you?

If you were fortunate in your search for a problution, you now have selected a means for resolving your problem. All you have to do is implement it and watch your problem situation be resolved. However, if you are like most people, you probably weren't quite so fortunate.

At the end of your search, you may have ended up with one final problution. A more common situation, however, is that you end up with one problution and then begin to see ways to modify it. You start playing around with it until, eventually, you end up with an entirely different problution. Or, you may end up with two or more problutions which appear to have almost equal potential to resolve your problem situation. If this occurs, you will have to make a decision about which will work best for you. Should you be unable to make such a decision, you then might consider possible ways of combining the two problutions into one workable problution.

A second likely outcome in your search for a problution involves implementation. Even if you have selected a final problution and are satisfied with it, you may find many obstacles to overcome before you can implement it. It doesn't matter how good a problution is. If you can't implement it successfully, it will have little value to you.

In the general Creative Problem-Solving (CPS) model (Parnes, Noller & Biondi, 1977; Isaksen & Treffinger, 1985), these two outcomes are dealt with using stages known as Solution-Finding and Acceptance-Finding. Both can be used after the hunt to help you select and implement problutions, should it be necessary. (Although the raw material used in the CPS model is ideas, the basic activities involved in processing ideas will be the same for problutions. In the discussion which follows, problutions will be substituted for ideas or options as typically used in the CPS model.)

Solution-Finding is designed to help you use criteria to screen, select, and support problutions you have found. Acceptance-Finding involves gaining acceptance for your problution (if needed) and developing a plan to insure successful implementation. As noted above, there may be situations in which you won't need to use either of these activities. There also may be just as many situations in which you will need to use either one or both of these stages. Since it is likely that you will need to use either Solution-Finding or Acceptance-Finding activities at some time, I will describe a generalized version of these two stages of the CPS model. For a more thorough and complete description, you should consult either of the references I cited previously.

Solution-Finding

If you end up with a large number of problutions and you want to reduce this number, you should screen out as many as possible. To do this, you will need to apply some general criteria (standards against which you can judge your problutions). First develop a list of the three most important criteria you can think of. Common examples are cost, time, and feasibility. Next, decide if each problution satisfies each criterion. For example, you might decide if a particular problution costs less than $100, would require no more than 20 minutes to implement, and has at least a 50-50 chance of resolving your problem situation. If any problution fails to satisfy these criteria, you might discard it. However, you also might want to consider ways to modify these problutions or combine them with others before you reject them. The screening process ends when you have reduced your list of problutions to what you consider to be a manageable number (e.g., three or four).

Selecting from a reduced list of problutions can be as simple as making an intuitive decision or as complex as using a matrix analysis with weighted criteria. If you believe a choice is evident to you and it "feels right," by all means go with it. However, before you make any quick decisions, consider the costs of things going wrong if you make a poor quality decision. If the time is available and the decision is important, you may want to use a more considered and analytical approach.

To select from among two to four problutions, you first should generate a list of as many possible criteria as you can think of. In doing this, it is important that you really try to "stretch" in coming up with a large number of criteria. Sometimes, failing to think of only one particular criterion can doom later implementation. The criterion you fail to consider might be the key to a high quality decision. Thus, you always should push for many different kinds of criteria.

Once you have generated your criteria list, you next should consider reducing the list in size. If you have the time and are motivated enough, you could consider using the entire list. However, there is no need to become obsessed in using a lengthy list. Sometimes, too many criteria can reduce decision quality as much as using too few criteria. In any event, you should use your final list of criteria to evaluate each of your remaining problutions. The problution which satisfies the most criteria can be selected for possible implementation.

Before you select a final problution, however, you might want to re-evaluate your reduced list of problutions to see if you can develop ways to support them. That is, you may want to "milk" each problution for any positive features before disposing of it. To do this, you can refer to your criteria and see if they suggest any ways to modify or improve any of the problutions before you reject them. Then you can begin the Acceptance-Finding stage.

Sometimes—no matter how conscientious you are

about combining or otherwise modifying problutions—you may find that you still can't choose the best problution to implement. Each appears to have different strengths and weaknesses, but it is difficult to systematically compare each problution against each strength and weakness. When this happens, you might try using a matrix with weighted criteria.

A matrix approach allows you to compare problutions and criteria in a systematic manner. Although this procedure will not completely eliminate subjectivity in your decision making, it at least will introduce a logical and practical means for making comparisons. In addition, assigning different weights to your criteria will take into account that some criteria can be more important to you than others. For example, when buying a new car, you probably would consider cost to be more important than the tread pattern on the tires (if you don't, I have a car I'd like to sell you).

To set up a matrix, use the rows to list problutions and the columns to list criteria. Next, weight the overall importance of each criterion. Use a five- or seven-point scale to do this. For example, you might use the following five-point scale to weight each criterion:

1 = No importance

2 = Low importance

3 = Medium importance

4 = High importance

5 = Very high importance

After weighting each criterion, you are ready to begin rating the problutions. To do this, you should rate each problution on the first criterion using a 1- 5-point scale. Isaksen and Treffinger (1985) suggest a scale such as the following:

1 = Unacceptable

2 = Needs improvement

3 = Satisfactory

4 = Very good

5 = Excellent

Then, rate each problution on the next criterion and so forth until you have rated each problution using each criterion. The next step is to multiply your weighting for each criterion by the rating you gave each problution for that criterion. Thus, if you weighted cost as a "5" and rated tire tread pattern as a "4," the product would be 20. Finally, add up all the products to obtain a total score for each problution.

An illustration of this process is shown in **Figure 9-1** using the example of the littering problem discussed in Chapter Five. The original problem in this situation was: IWWMW encourage people to stop littering the highways by throwing things out of their cars. Of the redefinitions I generated for this problem, I classified seven as problutions. As shown in **Figure 9-1**, I have selected three of them to illustrate the weighted matrix procedure: (1) IWWM airplanes and helicopters be used to catch people littering? (2) IWWM certain portions of highways be designated as areas for littering? (3) IWWM radar be used to detect littering of metallic material?

In **Figure 9-1**, I have listed three criteria across the top: "Low cost," "Few personnel" (number of personnel required to implement a problution), and "Successful" (how likely it is that a problution will resolve the problem). (in listing criteria, you should state them in terms of what you desire. Thus, you don't just want a problution to cost, but you want it to be low in cost.) I then assigned a subjective weight to each criterion and listed an abbreviated version of the three problutions down the left side. For the next step, I rated the airplanes, special areas, and radar on the criterion of cost and then did

Figure 9-1. Using a weighted matrix to select problutions.

Weightings:	Low Cost		Few Personnel		Successful		Totals
	5		3		5		Totals
1. Airplanes	2	10	5	15	3	15	40
2. Special areas	5	25	3	9	5	25	59
3. Radar	3	15	2	6	2	10	31

the same thing on the remaining two criteria. Finally, I multiplied each weighting factor times each rating score and added up the products across the criteria to obtain a total score. In this instance, setting up special areas just for littering received the highest score.

At this point, you might decide that you are unhappy with the outcome and decide to try again. If you are unhappy, you should re-assess all the weightings and ratings. You may decide to use different numbers. You also should determine if there might be some other criteria you neglected to include in your matrix. Leaving out one important criterion is all it takes sometimes to throw the whole process off (at least as far as our subjective perceptions are concerned). You also may decide to modify one or more of the problutions and begin the procedure again. Or, you even may want to reject all of the weighting results and start over using different problutions.

Acceptance-Finding

Once you have settled on a problution to implement, you can begin the final stage. As with Solution-Finding, this stage can be relatively easy or difficult to put into practice. It can be easy as jotting down a few things you need to do to gain acceptance of your problution and get it implemented; it can be as difficult as developing in-depth plans and contingency actions. The path you choose will depend upon your knowledge of the Acceptance-Finding process as well as the specifics of the problution you have selected and the environment in which you plan to implement it.

Implementation should proceed rather smoothly if your problution is relatively simple in structure (i.e., you clearly understand its major features), if the operations needed to help resolve your problem are fairly routine, and if there are few major obstacles. However, the reverse also can occur. Whenever a selected problution is complex in structure, implementation operations are ambiguous and nonroutine, and the environment is likely to resist implementation, you will need to devote some time and effort to generating a plan of action. This plan should be your goal in Acceptance-Finding.

Assuming you decide to do an intensive analysis in an attempt to insure successful implementation, you can start Acceptance-Finding. Begin by doing what is sometimes referred to as a "force-field" analysis of the problution's environment. That is, examine the factors which might assist or resist implementation. Isaksen and Treffinger (1985) suggest that you construct a grid with one column of "Assisters" and another column of "Resisters." Then, identify the Who? What? Where? When? Why? and How? elements of both the Assisters and the Resisters.

As an illustration, consider the problution of setting up special areas to be used by people who litter. An

Figure 9-2. Using Assisters and Resisters to develop a plan of action.

	ASSISTERS	RESISTERS
WHO (People)	Community groups, environmental groups, Highway maintenance dept.	People who litter, people who own the property, people near the areas
WHAT (Things)	Lots of trees to hide the litter, large amounts of litter in one location	Flat land where the wind would blow away a lot of the collected litter
WHERE (Places)	Areas far removed from towns, areas with easy access for litters	Areas inside of towns, areas with little access, areas far from highways
WHEN (Times)	Areas open 24 hours, have additional areas during special holidays	Areas near cities just starting a beautification program
WHY (Reasons)	Confines ugliness to a few areas, easier to pick up trash, less costly	People may not be motivated enough to use a special area
HOW (Actions)	Locate feasible areas, obtain community support, work with highway depts.	Highway official against a new idea, people refuse to go out of their way

analysis of this situation is shown in **Figure 9-2**. For each of the Who?, What?, Where?, When?, Why?, and How? questions, I have listed forces likely to assist or resist implementation. In looking over all of these forces, I then need to decide which ones are the most important. That is, I need to determine which elements I need to give the most attention when devising my plan of action.

In this case, I might decide that motivating people to use the special areas would be the greatest obstacle. My action plan would then involve generating ways to encourage people to confine their littering to certain locations. (Of course, I also might decide to redefine my problution or select another one.)

Looking over all the elements involved as Assisters and Resisters also can help me evaluate the likelihood of successful implementation. If the assisting forces appear to outweigh the resisting forces, then I can have some confidence that implementation will not be so difficult. However, if it appears that the resister forces have an overall advantage, implementation may be a little more difficult. In this instance, I would want to take special care in developing my action plan.

If I decide to proceed with the problution involving creation of special littering areas, I next should begin putting together my action plan. Isaksen and Treffinger (1985) suggest that this plan contain: (1) one or more immediate actions which can be completed within a 24-hour period, (2) a few short-term actions to be taken relatively soon, and (3) a few long-term actions. Also included with these long-term actions should be some thoughts on ways to evaluate the ongoing success of my plan.

For many situations, this three-part plan will be sufficient. A lot of problutions, however, will require that more attention be given to planning. Of particular concern is anticipating possible implementation blocks and devising ways to overcome them. A useful approach for doing this is Potential Problem Analysis (PPA) as described by Kepner and Tregoe (1981). The discussion which follows is based upon the Kepner and Tregoe model, but also includes modifications I have made (see, e.g., VanGundy, 1984). Here are the steps involved:

1. Generate a list of every possible problem which could develop when you try to implement your problution.

2. For each problem you have listed, think of every possible cause. That is, what could cause this problem to occur?

3. Using a four-point scale (1 = Unlikely, 2 = Moderately unlikely, 3 = Moderately likely, 4 = Likely), rate the likelihood of each problem and cause occurring.

4. Using a four-point scale (1 = Not at all serious, 2 = Somewhat serious, 3 = Serious, 4 = Disasterous), rate the degree of seriousness of each problem and cause occurring.

5. Develop one or more preventive actions for each problem and cause.

6. Using a four-point scale (1 = Unlikely, 2 = Moderately unlikely, 3 = Moderately likely, 4 = Likely), estimate the likelihood of each problem or cause still existing as an implementation block after you have applied the preventive actions. The resulting numbers are "residual probabilities."

7. (Optional) Multiply each seriousness rating (Step 4) by each residual probability rating (Step 6).

8. For each score obtained in Step 7 you consider to be "high," develop a contingency plan (a "high" score would be one that you judge to have both a high likelihood of still being a problem and to be a serious problem as well).

A sample PPA for the littering problem is shown in **Figure 9-3**. This example has been simplified considerably and would be more elaborate if I actually was trying to implement this problution. As can be seen in **Figure 9-3**, a contingency plan clearly appears to be indicated for

Figure 9-3. Example of a modified Potential Problem Analysis technique.

PROBLEM/CAUSES	P	S	PREVENTIVE ACTIONS	RP	SxRP
1. People not motivated to use areas	4	4	Award users with discount coupons for gasoline	2	8
a. Too far from highways	3	3	Build close to highways	1	3
b. Easier to throw trash out windows	4	4	Require violators to work on highway maintence	4	16
2. People unaware of areas	3	4	Saturate the media	2	8
a. Insufficient publicity	2	1	Notices on items likely to be littered	2	2
b. Signs on highway inadequate	3	3	Use more and larger signs	1	3

Note: P = Probability, S = Seriousness, RP = Residual Probability the obstacle where the Residual Probability times Seriousness score (RP x S) was 16. Generally speaking, you probably should develop such contingency plans whenever the costs involved in doing so are relatively low. A subproblem also might have to be dealt with in this case (e.g., IWWMW motivate people to defer throwing out their trash until they reach special littering areas?) Or, it may be that an entirely new problution will be needed.

At this point in the Acceptance-Finding process, you may feel that you have done all that you can to plan for implementation. If so, then you can begin to carry out your plan of action. Quite often, however, you still may have some doubt about how well you have anticipated every major implementation obstacle. If you experience such doubt, then you might try using an implementation checklist.

A simple, very basic checklist might be based upon the "Five W" and "How" questions. For example:

1. Who will implement the problution? Who will be responsible for different phases of implementation? Who will try to gain acceptance? Who will acquire any resources needed to implement the problution?

2. What will be implemented? What activities need to be carried out? What resources are needed to carry out the plan of action? What obstacles still need to be overcome?

3. Where will the plan be implemented? Where in the implementation process is the plan likely to encounter its most serious obstacle?

4. When will the plan be implemented? When is the best time to try overcoming each implementation obstacle? When is the last possible time before implementation that the plan of action can be revised if necessary?

5. Why is your plan of action likely to succeed? Why do you want to implement this particular problution? Why

should other people affected by the problution accept your plan of action?

6. How will you implement your problution to gain the best advantage for success? How likely is it that other people will accept your plan of action? How will others benefit from your plan? How should you try to "sell" your plan to others? How can you convince others that your plan is likely to succeed?

After dealing with these and any other questions you might think of, you have just about reached the end of the Acceptance-Finding stage. I say "just about " for two reasons.

First, all the stages of the CPS model are flexible and should not be viewed as discrete sets of activities. At any point during any one of the stages, you may find that you need to recycle to a previous stage or jump ahead to a following stage. As you encounter new information about your problem situation during Acceptance-Finding, you may decide to develop an entirely new plan of action or return to Solution-Finding and begin work on selecting a new problution.

A second reason you have "just about" reached the end of Acceptance-Finding is because Acceptance-Finding is a process and not a static activity. Even after you have implemented a problution, you will need to monitor its progress in resolving your original problem. You also should use the implementation process to provide yourself with feedback about how well you performed during Acceptance-Finding. In other words, you should make a conscious effort to learn from your experience. Such learning is a continuous activity and will not end upon completion of a formal problem-solving model.

REFERENCES

Amabile, T. M. *The social psychology of creativity.* New York: Springer-Verlag, 1983.

Beier, E. G. The effects of induced anxiety on flexibility of intellectual functioning. *Psychological Monographs,* 1951, *65 (326).*

Biondi, A. *The creative process.* Buffalo, NY: D.O.K., 1972.

Bloom, B. S. & Broder, L. J. *Problem solving processes of college students.* Chicago: University of Chicago Press, 1950.

Bourne, L. Y., Dominowski, R. L. & Loftus, E. F. *Cognitive processes.* Englewood Cliffs, NJ: Prentice-Hall, 1979.

Braybrooke, D. & Lindblom, C.E. *Strategy of decision.* New York: Free Press, 1963.

Castellan, N. J., Jr., Pisoni, D. B. & Potts, G. R. (Eds.). *Cognitive theory, volume 2.* Hillsdale, NJ: Lawrence Erlbaum Associates, 1977.

Cohen, M. D., March, J. G. & Olsen, J. P. A garbage can model of organizational choice. *Administrative Science Quarterly,* 1972, *17(1),* 1-25.

Crovitz, H. F. *Galton's walk.* New York: Harper & Row, 1970.

Csikszentmihalyi, M. & Getzels, J. W. Concern for discovery: An attitudinal component of creative production. *Journal of Personality,* 1970, *38(1),* 91-105.

Davis, M., McKay, M. & Eshelman, E. R. *The relaxation & stress reduction workbook.* Richmond, CA: New Harbinger Publications, 1980.

de Bono, E. *Lateral thinking: Creativity step by step.* New York: Harper & Row, 1970.

de Bono, E. *Lateral thinking for management.* New York: American Management Associations, 1971.

Dewey, J. The pattern of inquiry. *Logic: The structure of inquiry,* New York: Holt, 1938.

Dillon, J. T. Problem finding and solving. *The Journal of Creative Behavior,* 1982, *16,* 97-111.

Dollard, J. & Miller, N. E. *Personality and psychotherapy.* New York: McGraw-Hill, 1950.

Duncker, K. On problem solving. *Psychological Monographs,* 1945, *58(5),* Whole No. 270, 1-112.

D'Zurilla, T. J. & Goldfried, M. R. Problem solving and behavior modification. *Journal of Abnormal Psychology,* 1971, *78,(1),* 107-126.

Einstein, A. & Infeld, L. *The evolution of physics.* New York: Simon & Schuster, 1938.

Etzioni, A. *The active society.* New York: MacMillan, 1968.

Feldman, J. & Kanter, H. E. Organizational decision making. In J. G. March (Ed.), *Handbook of organizations.* Chicago: Rand McNally, 1965.

Frederikson, N. Implications of cognitive theory for instruction in problem solving. *Review of Educational Research,* 1984, *54(3),* 363-407.

Getzels, J. W. Problem finding. 343rd Convocation Address, *University of Chicago Record,* 1973, *1,* 281-283.

Getzels, J. W. Problem-finding and the inventiveness of solutions. *The Journal of Creative Behavior,* 1975, *9(1),* 12-18.

Getzels, J. W. Problem-finding and research in educational administration. In G. L. Immegart & W. L. Boyd (Eds.), *Problem-finding in educational administration.* Lexington, MA: Heath, 1979.

Getzels, J. W. & Csikszentmihalyi, M. *Creative thinking*

in art students: An exploratory study. Cooperative Research Report No. E-008, Chicago, 1964.

Getzels, J. W. & Csikszentmihalyi, M. *Creative thinking in art students: The process of discovery.* Cooperative Research Report No. 9080. Chicago, 1965.

Getzels, J. W. & Cskiszentmihalyi, M. From problem solving to problem finding. In I. A. Taylor & J. W. Getzels (Eds.) *Perspectives in creativity.* Chicago: Aldine, 1975.

Gordon, W. J. J. *Synectics.* New York: Harper & Row, 1961.

Grandori, H. A prescriptive contingency view of organizational decision making. *Administrative Science Quarterly,* 1984, *29,* 192-209.

Greeno, J. G. Indefinite goals in well-structured problems. *Psychological Reports,* 1976, *83,* 479-491.

Greeno, J. G. Process of understanding in problem solving. In N. J. Castellan, Jr., D. B. Pisoni & G. R. Potts (Eds.), *Cognitive theory, volume 2.* Hillsdale, NJ: Lawrence Erlbaum Associates, 1977.

Grossman, S. R. Releasing problem solving energies. *Training and Development Journal.* 1984, *38(5),* 94-98.

Heppner, P. P. Personal problem solving: A descriptive study of individual differences. *Journal of Counseling Psychology,* 1982, *29(6),* 580-590.

Heppner, P. P., Hibel, J., Neal, G. W., Weinstein, C. L. & Rabinowitz, F. E. Personal problem solving: A descriptive study of individual differences. *Journal of Counseling Psychology,* 1982, *29(6),* 580-590.

Heppner, P. P. & Peterson, C. H. The development and implications of a personal problem-solving inventory. *Journal of Counseling Psychology,* 1982, *29(1),* 66-75.

Hirschman, E. C. Some novel propositions concerning problem solving. *IEEE Engineering Management,* 1982, *10,* 47-56.

Holsti, K. J. Resolving international conflicts: A taxonomy of behavior and some figures on procedures. *Journal of Conflict Resolution*, 1966, *10*, 272-296.

Isaksen, S. G. & Treffinger, D. J. *Creative problem solving: The basic course*. Buffalo, NY: Bearly Limited, 1985.

Isenberg, D. J. How senior managers think. *Harvard Business Review*, 1984, *62(6)*, 81-90.

Kaplan, R. E. Creativity in the everyday business of managing. *Issues & Observations*, Greensboro, NC: Center for Creative Leadership, 1983, *3(2)*, 1-6.

Kepner, C. H. & Tregoe, B. B. *The new rational manager*. Princeton, NJ: Kepner-Tregoe, 1981.

Larkin, J., McDermott, J., Simon, D. P & Simon, H.A. Expert and novice performance in solving physics problems. *Science*, 1980, *208*, 1335-1342.

Levine, S. Stress and behavior. *Scientific American*, 1971, *224*, 26-31.

Lloyd, I. Don't define the problem. *Public Administration Review*, 1978, *38,*283-286.

Lyles, M. A. & Mitroff, I. I. Organizational problem formulation: An empirical study. *Administrative Science Quarterly*, 1980, *25*, 102-119.

MacCrimmon, K. R. Managerial decision making. In J. W. McGuire (Ed.), *Contemporary management, issues and viewpoints*. Englewood Cliffs, NJ: Prentice-Hall, 1974.

MacCrimmon, K. R. & Taylor, R. N. Decision making and problem solving. In M. D. Dunnette (ed.), *Handbook of industrial and organizational psychology*, Chicago: Rand McNally, 1976.

Mackworth, N. H. Orginality. *American Psychologist*, 1965, *20*, 51-66.

Maier, N. R. F. Reasoning in humans. II. The solution of a problem and its appearance in consciousness.

Journal of Comparative Psychology, 1931, *13,* 181-194.

Maier, N. R. F. *Problem solving discussions and conferences: Leadership methods and skills.* New York: McGraw-Hill, 1963.

Moore, M. T. The relationship between the originality of essays and variables in the problem-discovery process: A study of creative and noncreative middle school students. *Research in the Teaching of English,* 1985, *19(1),* 84-95.

Mowrer, O. H. *Learning theory and the symbolic processes,* New York: Wiley, 1960.

Newell, A., Shaw, J. C. & Simon, H. A. Chess-Playing programs and the problem of complexity. *IBM Journal of Research Development,* 1958, *2,* 320-335.

Newell, A. & Simon, H. A. *Human problem solving.* Englewood Cliffs, NJ: Prentice-Hall, 1972.

Noller, R. B. *Scratching the surface of creative problem-solving: A bird's eye-view of CPS.* Buffalo, NY: D.O.K., 1977.

Olson, R. W. *The art of creative thinking.* New York: Barnes & Noble, 1980.

O'Toole, J. *Work in America.* Cambridge, MA: Institute of Technology Press, 1972.

Parnes, S. J., Noller, R. B. & Biondi, A. M. *Guide to creative action (rev. ed.).* New York: Charles Scribner's, 1977.

Perfetto, G. A., Bransford, J. D. & Franks, J. J. Constraints on access in a problem solving context. *Memory and Cognition,* 1983, *11,* 24-31.

Pounds, W. F. Processes of problem-finding. *Industrial Management Review,* 1969, *11,* 1-19.

Prince, G. M. *The practice of creativity.* New York: Harper and Row, 1970.

Prince, G. M. The mindspring theory: A new development from Synectics research. *The Journal of Creative Behavior,* 1975, *9,* 159-181.

Reitman, W. R. *Cognition and thought.* New York: John Wiley, 1965.

Reitman, W. R. Heuristic decision procedures, open constraints, and the structure of ill-defined problems. In M. W. Shelly, III & G. L. Bryan (Eds.), *Human judgments and optimality.* New York: John Wiley, 1964.

Ritchey, K. M., Carscaddon, D. M. & Morgan, C. H. Problem-solving appraisal versus hypothetical problem solving. *Psychological Reports,* 1984, *55,* 815-818.

Rubinstein, M. F. Problem solving on both sides of the brain. *IEEE Engineering Management,* 1982, *10(1),* 82-85.

Shaftel, F. R. & Shaftel, G. *Role playing for social values: Decision making in the social studies.* Englewood Cliffs, NJ: Prentice-Hall, 1967.

Simon, H. A. The structure of ill-structured problems. *Artificial Intelligence,* 1973, *4,* 181-201.

Simon, H. A. A behavioral model of rational choice. *Quarterly Journal of Economics,* 1955, *69,* 99-118.

Sims, D. A framework for understanding the definition and formulation of problems in teams. *Human Relations,* 1979, *32,* 909-921.

Skinner, B. F. *Science and human behavior.* New York: Macmillan, 1953.

Smilansky, J. Problem solving and the quality of invention: An empirical investigation. *Journal of Educational Psychology,* 1984, *76(3),* 377-386.

Sprecher, T. B. Chairman's report on criteria of creativity at Third Utah Conference, 1959. Cited by Anne Roe in Psychological approaches to creativity in science. In M. A. Coler (Ed.), *Essays on creativity in the sciences.* New York: New York University Press, 1963.

Sweller, J. Control mechanisms in problem solving. *Memory and Cognition.* 1983, *11*, 32-40.

Sweller, J. & Levine, M. Effects of goal specificity on means-end analysis and learning. *Journal of Experimental Psychology: Learning, Memory, and Cognition,* 1982, *8*, 463-474.

Taylor, R. N. Nature of ill-structuredness: Implications for problem formulation and solution. *Decision Sciences,* 1974, *5*,632-643.

Thelen, H. A. *Education and the human quest (2nd ed.).* Chicago: University of Chicago Press, 1972.

Tuma, D. T. & Reif, F. (Eds.). *Problem solving and education: Issues in teaching and research.* Hillsdale, NJ: Lawrence Erlbaum Associates, 1980.

VanGundy, A. B. *Techniques of structured problem solving, 2nd ed.* New York: Van Nostrand Reinhold, 1988.

VanGundy, A. B. *108 ways to get a bright idea and increase your creative potential.* Englewood Cliffs, NJ: Prentice-Hall, 1983.

VanGundy, A. B. *Managing group creativity: A modular approach to problem solving.* New York: AMACOM, 1984.

Wallas, G. *The art of thought.* New York: Harcourt, 1926.

Watzlawick, P., Weakland, J. & Fisch, R. *Change, principles of problem formation and problem resolution.* New York: W. W. Norton, 1974.

Wertheimer, M. *Productive thinking* (Enl. Ed.). New York: Harper & Row, 1959.

BIBLIOGRAPHY

Bouchard, T. J. & Drauden, G. Discovery-oriented behavior and problem solving. *The Journal of Psychology*, 1976, *92*, 243-248.

Carroll, J. M., Miller, L. A., Thomas, J. C. & Friedman, H. P. Aspects of solution structure in design problem solving. *American Journal of Psychology*, 1980, *93(2)*, 269-284.

Glick, M. L. & Holyoak, K. J. Analogical problem solving. *Cognitive Psychology*, 1980, *12*, 306-35.

Glaser, R. Education and thinking: The role of knowledge. *American Psychologist*, 1984, *39(2)*, 39-104.

Henle, M. The snail beneath the shell. *Abraxas*, 1971, *1(2)*, 119-133.

Heppner, P. P., Neal, G. W. & Larson, L. M. Problem-solving training as prevention with college students. *Personnel and Guidance Journal*, 1984, *62(9)*, 514-519.

Kant, E. & Newell, A. Problem solving techniques for the design of algorithms. *Information Processing and Management*, 1984, *20(12)*, 97-118.

Larson, L. M. & Heppner, P. P. The relationship of problem-solving appraisal to career decision and indecision. *Journal of Vocational Behavior*, 1985, *26*, 55-65.

Livingston, S. Myth of the well-educated manager. *Harvard Business Review*, 1971, *49*, 79-89.

Nezu, A. & D'Zurilla, T. J. Effects of problem definition and formulation on decision making in the social problem-solving process. *Behavior Therapy*, 1981, *12*, 100-106.

Noble, C. E. Solving ill-structured management problems. *Business*, 1979, *29*, 26-33.

Nutt, P. C. Types of organizational decision processes. *Administrative Science Quarterly*, 1984, *29*, 414-450.

Phillips, S. D., Pazienza, N. J. & Ferrin, H. H. Decision-making styles and problem-solving appraisal. *Journal of Counseling Psychology*, 1984, *31(4)*, 497-502.

Schubert, D. S. P. Increase in creativity by prior response to a problem. *Journal of General Psychology*, 1977, *96*, 323-324.

Schwenk, C. R. Laboratory research on ill-structured decision aids: The case of dialectical inquiry. *Decision Sciences*, 1983, *14(1)*, 140-144.

Simon, H. A. Discovery, invention, and devlopment: Human creative thinking. *Proceedings of the National Academy of Science, USA*, 1983, *80*, 4569-4571.

Solem, A. R. The effect of situational vs. behavioral problem statements on solution quality. *Human Relations*, 1976, *29(3)*, 249-255.